Karaoke Idols

Karaoke Idols

Popular Music and the Performance of Identity

Dr. Kevin Brown

Afterword by Philip Auslander

intellect Bristol, UK / Chicago, USA

First published in the UK in 2015 by
Intellect, The Mill, Parnall Road, Fishponds, Bristol, BS16 3JG, UK

First published in the USA in 2015 by
Intellect, The University of Chicago Press, 1427 E. 60th Street,
Chicago, IL 60637, USA

A catalogue record for this book is available from the British Library.

Copy-editor: MPS Technologies
Cover designer: Shin-E Chuah
Production manager: Claire Organ
Typesetting: Contentra Technologies

Print ISBN: 978-1-78320-444-1
ePDF ISBN: 978-1-78320-445-8
ePUB ISBN: 978-1-78320-446-5

For Grandpa Jim. We did it!

Contents

Acknowledgments

An enormous thank you to all of the wonderful people who have helped me with this project. Parts of this book were presented at academic conferences including Performance Studies International, the Association for Theatre in Higher Education, the International Association of Popular Music Studies, the Association for Asian Performance, and the Association of Asian Studies. Thanks to the panel chairs, fellow participants, and attendees for their input. Portions of Chapter 3 originally appeared in *Popular Music Studies* 26: 1 (2014). Portions of Chapter 5 originally appeared in *Popular Entertainment Studies* 1: 2 (2010). I thank these journals for their permission to reprint this material. I would like to thank the professors of my doctoral committee for all of their input, including my advisor Oliver Gerland, second reader Paul Shankman, Bud Coleman, Beth Osnes, and Merrill Lessley. Thank you to Phil Auslander for your inspiration, input, and contribution. Thank you to Claire Organ and Jelena Stanovnik at Intellect Books, and MPS Technologies, for all of your help to bring this project to publication. Thanks to the James R., Anne M., and R. Jane Emerson Student Support Fund in the Humanities for your generous support during my research. Thanks to Marcy, Tod, Paul, and Nancy. Thank you to my wife Lauren for helping me find my way. Thanks to all of the wonderful people at 'Capone's'. You will always be in my heart!

Synopsis

For two years toward the end of the 2000s, I performed ethnographic research at a karaoke bar near Denver, Colorado, in the United States. When I say that I performed, I mean I performed karaoke. Over the course of two years, I went from wallflower to local celebrity. When I started, I could hardly carry a tune. By the time my research ended, people were putting in requests for songs that they wanted to hear me sing. Karaoke taught me a lot about myself, teaching me how to be more confident and how to better relate to other people. This book is the story about how this happened. It is also the story about why this happened, about the countless other people who I witnessed sing, and about how our identities are shaped through the microcosmic interactions of everyday life. The book begins by introducing the reader to the purpose of the book, which is to use karaoke performances as a window into understanding how human identity is constructed. Chapter 1 lays the groundwork for the methodology used in the project, including a discussion of ethnographic research tools based in performance ethnography, including participant observation, auto-ethnography, thick description, and embodied writing. Chapter 2 explores the history of karaoke within the context of Japanese culture. Chapters 3 through 5 use karaoke performances as examples to discuss the construction of categories of identity: gender, ethnicity, and class. Chapter 6 synthesizes the discussion, concluding that performances of individual identity coalesce to form performances of community. The book concludes that karaoke provides a space of cultural production where performances of identity are not only constructed, but also subverted. Human identity is constructed through small performances that occur all around us in everyday life.

Synopsis

[illegible]

About the Author

Dr. Kevin Brown is an Assistant Professor of Digital Media and Performance Studies in the Department of Theatre at the University of Missouri, Columbia, MO, United States. He has been a producer, director, actor, and designer of theater for twenty-five years. He is an editorial review board member of the *International Journal of Performance Arts and Digital Media*. Brown currently serves on the Board of Directors of Performance Studies International as their Digital Publications Officer. He has published many works, including 'Liveness Anxiety: Karaoke and the Performance of Class' in *Popular Entertainment Studies*, 'Auslander's Robot' and 'The Auslander Test: Or, "Of Bots and Humans"' in the *International Journal of Performance Arts and Digital Media*, 'Spectacle as Resistance: Performing Tree Ordination in Thailand' in the *Journal of Religion and Theatre*, 'Dancing into the Heart of Darkness: Modern Variations and Innovations of the Thai Shadow Theatre' in *Puppetry International*, 'European Theatre and Performance' in the *Encyclopedia of World Popular Culture*, and entries on karaoke, interactive video games, national identity, virtual bands, virtual communities, and social networks in *Music in American Life: An Encyclopedia of the Songs, Styles, Stars, and Stories that Shaped Our Culture*. His article 'Sometimes a Microphone is Just a Microphone: Karaoke and the Performance of Gender' was recently published in *Popular Music Studies.*

About the Author

Overture

It starts out as a fairly mellow Saturday night at Capone's. Several of the regular singers are performing their trademark songs. Jennifer is a young woman in her early twenties with a pale complexion, long brown hair, and a petite frame. She wears clothes that are typical of an average working-class girl of her age: a white blouse with thin, blue, horizontal stripes, blue jeans, and plain black leather shoes. She has chosen to sing 'She's in Love With the Boy,' as written by John Simms and recorded by Trisha Yearwood. Jennifer arrived earlier in the night with her boyfriend, a young, short-haired man dressed in a white, long-sleeve shirt, blue jeans, and cowboy boots. He admires her performance from his seat on a stool by one of the pool tables near the back of the bar. The song is about a young girl who is in love with a boy of whom her father does not approve. Their eyes meet as she sings, a demonstration of the performance of a gendered relationship.

As Jennifer wraps up her song, a group of young men in their twenties enters the bar, a common event late at night when the mood at the bar goes from subdued to raucous, as the older regulars filter home, replaced with younger patrons who often arrive at karaoke later in the night after attending various concerts or parties. Among the new arrivals is Kenny, a young Latino man in his early twenties. He wears a black concert T-shirt with red lettering, baggy blue jeans, and tennis shoes. His hair is shaggy, and he wears a dark goatee and a thin mustache on his face. He also sports multiple piercings, including an eyebrow ring, a small gold nose ring, and large hoop earrings in both of his ears. He has several small, colorful tattoos along his forearms. Kenny turns in a slip of paper to the Karaoke Jockey (KJ) and soon he is called up to sing. He has chosen to sing the song 'Poison,' by Bell Biv Devoe. He sprints up to the stage and grabs the microphone. The voice that comes out of his mouth is a bit surprising for his tattooed and pierced appearance: it is soft, somewhat fey and lisping. But the words are not as soft, and he bellows into the microphone as he starts his song: 'Less fuckin' country!'

Kenny sings the song loudly, dancing from side-to-side with one arm holding the mike and the other arm held in a fist, pumping it up and down. After Kenny is done, he goes back to his group of friends who are hanging out along the back wall of the bar, giving him 'high fives' as he returns to his seat. After Kenny, it is Jennifer's turn to sing again. This time she is singing 'Crazy,' a song that was written by Willie Nelson and made famous by Patsy Cline. As she begins to sing, Kenny starts to taunt her. 'That's not how it goes,' he shouts at her, 'you're fucking it up!' Jennifer is visibly shaken and tries to ignore Kenny. Kenny begins to sing along with Jennifer from the audience, trying to correct her, and she gestures to him with her middle finger. During the next musical break, Jennifer looks at Kenny, then points to her boyfriend and threatens him, 'That's my boyfriend. He's gonna kick your ass if you don't shut up!' Kenny backs off for the moment, but the mood among the rest of the patrons in the bar has perceptibly shifted from mellow to tense. Eventually, the situation seems to be diffused through the fact that it is happening in the public context of a karaoke performance and not in private. As far as I can tell, no actual violence happens and all of the parties involved in this verbal (and musical) scuffle go home unscathed.

The Big Three Killed My Baby

This performance was one of many I observed during my ethnographic research of a local karaoke bar. How is it that three words directed at a genre of music ('Less Fuckin' Country') could create so much trouble? The answer to this question seems to be rooted in the way that karaoke, as a space of cultural production, acts as a conduit for the performance of various categories of human identity. This particular example is quite unique, in that it involves all three of the categories of the performance of identity that will be examined in this study: gender, ethnicity, and class.

I ask you, the reader, to answer this question, did the conflict in this example arise because of tensions due to: (A) gender, (B) ethnicity, (C) class, or (D) all of the above? It might seem that, in this example, the performances of these various categories of identity are hopelessly entangled. If so, how does one go about untangling them? The purpose of this research is to use karaoke as a window into discussing the formation of human identity; to interrogate the means by which social categories of identity – especially gender, ethnicity, and class – are constructed through performances; and to document the ways karaoke can be used to subvert these fabrications.

After all, what do we know, on a microscopic level, about the formation of identity? Much has been written in contemporary academic discourse about 'constructions,' and especially about the construction of 'identity,' but not much has been written about how exactly the constructions are, for lack of a better term, constructed. In this book, I use karaoke performances to show how the missing ingredient in discourses about identity is a deeper understanding of performance itself: how performance acts construct categories of human identity. Furthermore, this book discusses issues at the forefront of contemporary culture: the intersection of technology and culture, our society's fascination with celebrity, and the perceived notion that the new media is leading to a loss of community.

Beyond the 'big three' categories of identity, performances of identity extend to other categories as well, such as nationality, religion, age, and so on. Moreover, the performance of identity contributes to the formation of human agency and community. In addition to questions about the performance of identity, this book will discuss other issues that have emerged from this study. For example, what is the relationship between the performance of karaoke in America and the performance of karaoke in other countries, and particularly in the county of its origin, Japan? Are there variations of the performance of karaoke within regions or cultural geographies that create subcultures of karaoke performers? What is the relationship between karaoke and a postmodern, mediatized twenty-first century culture? What does the phenomenon of karaoke say about human nature? Why is karaoke so popular on a global and universal level? What functions does karaoke play in society? This book is an attempt to forge new tools that will help to answer these questions.

This ethnography has been written in a way meant to appeal to both an academic and general audience. Thus, it is my hope that it will bring an awareness and understanding of academic discourse, especially relating to issues about identity, outside of the academy. Understanding the performance of gender, ethnicity, and class is extremely important, because it helps people look beyond 'naturalized' notions of these categories of identity, and helps people understand how these categories are cultural and not due to genetic factors. A deeper understanding of these topics can potentially lead to less sexism, racism, and classism in our society. In addition, this book uses a new approach to ethnography, and is a blueprint for exiting new studies about contemporary popular culture. Topics related to popular culture are often ignored in academic circles because they are looked down upon as 'lowbrow,' and thus not worthy of academic study. This academic bias leaves great swaths of our culture understudied and misunderstood.

This study is especially notable, in that the methodologies employed demonstrate a way around criticisms that traditional ethnographic research is entrenched in a colonial model. Learning about what makes karaoke so popular holds important lessons, not only for social scientists, but also for aspiring entrepreneurs and business people. Karaoke is a multibillion dollar industry that has had very little study from an academic perspective. The intersection of technology and culture provides an example of the ways that digital media are shaping our society in new ways. Subcultures created around karaoke performances give us hints about how technology and the new media are enabling a new means for the formation of human communities. The ubiquity of karaoke in the media has to do with its appeal as a cauldron for the formation of identity and the universal human desire for celebrity. This book proposes that the dream of celebrity is rooted in a desire to replace a sense of community that has been lost in contemporary culture.

By using karaoke as a context to discuss the intersection of performance and everyday life, it is my goal to give the reader a deeper understanding of the way performances affect the way we think about categories of human identity, and the way that performances of identity are translated into performances of community. Through sharing my own personal journey, I hope to share the way I have come to see the world as full of performances. I see performances all around me, in art and in life.

Chapter 1

My Way

For what is a man, what has he got?
If not himself, then he has naught.

– Paul Anka

The descriptions of karaoke performances in this book are accounts of real events that I observed during an ethnographic study of a karaoke bar near Denver, Colorado, in the United States. To ensure that privacy is respected, all of the names used in this book are completely fictionalized. However, all of the performances that I write about are entirely real. I have strived to capture as much detail as possible from my original experiences in order to give the reader a feeling for what it was like to be in my shoes, observing and participating in these performances. 'Capone's' is the fictional name of a real place, a fairly typical local bar. I picked this particular research site because of the diversity of the people who frequent it. Capone's is a place where the white-collar collides with the blue-collar, the straight mingle with the gay, and people of all colors drink their beer and whiskey side by side. It is a great place to observe many kinds of performances by many kinds of people. Over the course of several years, from 2007 to 2009, I visited Capone's on a regular basis, an average of once a week. On an average night, I would sing three or more songs. Usually, there were between five to ten other singers in the rotation. So, over the course of my study, I performed hundreds of times, and I watched thousands of karaoke performances. The descriptions of karaoke performances in this book, and the theoretical discussions that surround them, were born out of these experiences.

The Colorado suburb where I undertook this study, while perhaps not as diverse as the average community in America, is a relatively multicultural city compared to other municipalities in the same county. The amount of diversity among the patrons who come to inhabit Capone's on karaoke night seems to reflect these numbers. In fact, because of the wide variety of the types of people there, it is impossible to use a stereotypical label to describe the bar (such as 'Sports Bar,' 'Blue-Collar Bar,' or 'Yuppie Bar'). On any given night, it can be any one of these, or all of these, depending on the season of the year, the day of the week, and the time of day. During the daylight hours, it is a family restaurant where one can order everything from typical American cuisine, such as steak, hamburgers, hot dogs, and cheese fries, to the slightly eclectic, including burritos, gyros, and fish and chips. After dinner time, the family clientele slowly drain out the door, and a more typical bar crowd begins to arrive, changing over from the after-work happy-hour crowd to the serious full-time drinkers who inhabit their bar stools until last call. This diversity is what makes this location such a rich site to observe karaoke. The clientele is very diverse in terms of economic class, age, gender, and ethnicity. At various karaoke nights, I have met a thirty-something single male attorney, an octogenarian Italian immigrant who fought in World War II, a twenty-something female steel worker/single mother of three, as well as a migrant farm worker whom I spoke to at length in Spanish. In the end, I chose Capone's as a site for my research because it is a great place to observe many kinds of performances by many kinds of people.

Setting the Stage

The atmosphere at Capone's is fairly low-key. Christmas lights adorn almost every ceiling beam and arched doorway throughout the bar. These lights bathe the karaoke performers in a warm glow of soft reds, greens, yellows, and blues. The walls of the bar are covered in green wallpaper with gold and lavender fringes. Framed newspaper clippings about bank robberies and black-and-white photographs of depression-era Chicago line the walls of the bar, around the two sections that contain the pool tables and along the hallways that lead to the bathrooms. These photographs and news items vaguely allude to what could be considered the theme of the bar/restaurant: an exploration of the 'outlaw' archetype.

Apart from these framed items, the primary decoration of the bar is commercial advertising of various sorts. This includes neon signs hawking various brands of alcohol including beer, vodka, rum, and whisky, as well as advertisements for cigarettes and energy drinks. This pastiche of capitalism contributes to setting a very curious kind of scene in which the spectacle of commercialism is simultaneously at the forefront but also invisible because of its ubiquity, the sea of advertisements comprising a totalized hegemony to the casual observer. The onslaught is so overwhelming that the various commercials blend together in their entirety, and it becomes a kind of background of gray noise. This deluge of colorful advertising is one of the things that unmistakably marks Capone's as a site of commerce. It is a site of commerce in more than one way. Every night there is an exchange of goods in the form of hard-earned cash and credit cards swiped in return for food, drinks, and fun. But there is also an exchange of goods on another level, more along the lines of what might be described as 'meat market' commerce, that is, the possibility in the air of the exchange of a more romantic nature as well. It is among the performance of these exchanges that various categories of identity are constructed.

At Capone's, there are two nights of the week dedicated to karaoke, Wednesdays and Saturdays. Each night has a different Karaoke Jockey. Wednesday's KJ, Ron, is an older man in his sixties. Ron is 'old school,' and runs his karaoke show with a collection of hundreds of CD+Gs (compact discs with graphics), that he houses in binders that he sets up each night on a table along the wall behind his soundboard. The Saturday KJ is Tom, a middle-aged man in his early fifties. Tom's setup is all digital, consisting of thousands of songs that he keeps on his laptop, sometimes prone to computer errors.

I prefer to sing on Wednesdays, because it is less crowded and I get to sing more often. This is the same reason why most of the regulars prefer to sing on Wednesdays. In addition, Wednesday's audience is usually more attentive to the singing. Many times, and more often on Saturday nights, I get the feeling that as I perform I might as well be a recorded voice on the juke box in the corner of the room. Some of my favorite karaoke memories, nonetheless, are made on Saturday nights when I overcome all of the technical difficulties and apathy, and have a bar full of people singing along with me.

Saturday nights and Wednesday nights each have their own type of crowd. Wednesday nights are more subdued, and thus attract more of the 'regulars.' Saturday nights attract more of what the regulars call 'tourists,' the people who show up at Capone's on any one given night and then are never seen again. Many of the tourists are there for parties of various kinds, the most popular being birthday parties, followed closely behind by wedding celebrations (bachelor and bachelorette parties and post-reception parties), and anniversary parties. The tension between the regulars and the tourists is often palpable, mostly because the regulars take karaoke seriously and the tourists, more often, do not.

Steppin' Out

When I first began to go out to observe karaoke performances, I was terrified of singing. Before I began my study, I had only sung karaoke once, during the late 1980s. My girlfriend at the time and I attended a stand-up comedy show in Colorado Springs, the city where I grew up. After the show, as we walked into the lobby, we saw that they had a small stage set up for karaoke. My girlfriend and I had met in high school when she was performing Dorothy in *The Wizard of Oz*, and I was a techie on the same show. I suggested that she should sing, since I knew she was a very good singer. She replied, 'Only if you sing first.' So, I took her up on her dare, and picked out the song 'Welcome to the Jungle' by Guns N' Roses. At this point in my life, the only time I had sung in public before was in church. The song proved to be way out of my singing range. Since most of the lyrics are screamed, I did well enough to get a positive reaction from the audience. After I was done, I said 'Now it's your turn.' Although my girlfriend attempted to back out of the deal we had made, I eventually convinced her to sing. When she finally got on stage, she did an incredible version of 'Over the Rainbow.' The audience enjoyed her performance so much that they made her do an encore.

Between that date in the summer of 1988 and the summer of 2007, I did not sing any karaoke. Even during the first phase of my study, when I was scouting possible sites for my study, I would sit quietly in the audience, but I would not sing. I have found that this is a very common phenomenon. I have encountered many people who go to karaoke every week, but never sing. They all have their own litany of excuses, the most popular being, 'Trust me, you don't want to hear me sing.' Perhaps I, like many people in our society, have been conditioned to think that performance is not something that the untrained 'masses' should attempt. We are convinced that we should let the 'artists' create art. Or, perhaps it was my own insecurity about my voice. I have been an actor for many years, so I am very accustomed to stage fright, but for some reason, it took me quite a while to overcome my fear of singing on stage.

In the book *Karaoke Nights: An Ethnographic Rhapsody* (2001), communications scholar Robert Drew explains the difficulties associated with singing karaoke. He quotes one of the singers that he encountered in his study: 'It's the rawest form of performing you can do' (Drew 2001: 36). Besides the many possibilities of technical difficulties that can occur during a performance, there is also the problem that, very often, the arrangement of the karaoke version of the song is quite different from the original recording. To make matters worse, different versions of the same song might be recorded in different keys. Thus, one might think that a song is within his or her vocal range, but then encounter a karaoke version of the song that has been recorded in a key higher or lower than the original version. Drew points out that professional singers are in complete control of the conditions of their performances: 'Famous singers (and famous people who feel inclined to sing) can have their background music tailored to their competencies and their characters. A nicely recorded backdrop can flatter even the narrowest voice, as is proven, for instance, by Ringo Starr's many hits. As Steve Jones writes "The ability to record sound is power over sound"' (Jones qtd. in Drew 2001: 36). The conditions of the karaoke performance, on the other hand, are far beyond the control of the singer. This is what makes it so intimidating. I have seen trained singers who have excellent voices go down in flames, or just refuse to sing because of the difficulty of the performance conditions.

When I finally got up the nerve to sing, I found the experience exhilarating but also humbling. During the course of my study, I 'bombed' many times. When I first started, I could not carry a tune in a bucket. I often found that I thought that I knew a song much better than I actually did. Figuring out exactly how the mechanics of the karaoke machine worked was also a daunting task. The words of the lyrics to the song are displayed on the screen, but the exact timing and harmony are not. Sometimes unexpected and distracting things happen on the video track, such as images that seem arbitrarily paired with the song, or places where the words to the song have obviously been 'lost in translation.' But I did not let my failures get me down. Every time I sang, I got better. By the time I was finishing up my study in the spring of 2009, I can honestly say that I had become quite a good singer, and I had left my previous stage fright behind.

Karaoke Ethnography

To my knowledge, there has never been an ethnography on the subject of karaoke quite like this one. There have been ethnographies written dedicated to the topic of karaoke, but none of them have been conducted with a focus on performance, and none of them have been focused on one particular site over an interval of two years. Studies on karaoke have been conducted by researchers from various fields, including communication studies (Lum

1996, Drew 2001), anthropology (Kelly 1997), and sociology (De Nora 2000). This is the first in-depth ethnographic study of karaoke to be undertaken in over a decade.

The first ethnography on the subject of karaoke to be published was Casey Man Kong Lum's *In Search of a Voice: Karaoke and the Construction of Identity in Chinese America* (1996). In this book, Lum writes about karaoke from a communication studies perspective. His ethnography includes three sections, focused on a Cantonese Opera festival in New York's Chinatown, a karaoke party in an affluent Taiwanese suburb in New Jersey, and a community of Malaysian-Chinese immigrants singing karaoke at a restaurant in Flushing, New York.

The second ethnography to be published on the subject of karaoke, and one as groundbreaking as Lum's, is Robert Drew's *Karaoke Nights: An Ethnographic Rhapsody* (2001). Drew studied numerous karaoke bars in Philadelphia, New York, and Florida. Over the course of six years, Drew went to karaoke bars 'on about 140 occasions at 30 different bars' (Drew 2001: 26). Thus, although Drew and I have probably gone to a similar number of karaoke nights, Drew did this in a variety of locations. Although I scouted a score of karaoke bars during the first phase of my project, my two years 'in the field' were spent at one location, making my study the most in-depth ethnography of a single karaoke performance venue undertaken thus far.

One of the very first scholarly articles about karaoke was published in 1994, titled 'Karaoke: Subjectivity, Play and Interactive Media,' by Johan Fornäs, a musicologist. In this article, Fornäs describes several of his own encounters with karaoke in Sweden. Fornäs begins his article with what seems to be a variation of the same thesis with which I started. He conjectures, 'It would be interesting to study karaoke producers' choice of songs, as well as the selections purchased by different groups of consumers (private persons, clubs, bars, restaurants, etc.) and the selections made by different groups of users/performers (by gender, age, socio-economic classes, ethnic groups, etc.)' (Fornäs 1994: 91).

Fornäs suggests that ethnography would be a good way to study karaoke. He predicts, 'Here we need more detailed ethnographic user studies, which should also analyze the socio-demographic consumption of various user and consumer groups in terms of sex, age, ethnicity, locality, and class' (Fornäs 1994: 98). Fornäs also suggests that karaoke is the perfect medium in which to study the performance of subjectivity. He explains, 'By trying on Madonna's or Michael Jackson's provocative style of expression, Sinatra's maturity or Sid Vicious' cynical brutality, one might discover new potentials in oneself, in the modes of expression and in friends' response' (Fornäs 1994: 96). Thus, it seems that I am not the only one who has been drawn to the study of karaoke as a way to explore how people perform identities.

Smells Like Teen Spirit

At the beginning of my study, one of the biggest shocks to my system was the realization of how late at night karaoke takes place. Although many karaoke nights begin at *maybe* 8:00 p.m., most of the people who sing do not arrive until about 9:00 p.m. on the weekends and about 10:00 p.m. or later on weeknights. As an aging scholar, these late nights were immediately a challenge to my constitution. In fact, it made me painfully aware of how old I am (although I am only approaching middle age), at least in comparison to the majority of the people out that late at night, most of who are in their mid-twenties. Soon, I found myself taking naps on the days that I sang karaoke, and arranging to sleep in on the days after. On a typical outing, I would take a nap from about 4:00 to 7:00 p.m., wake up, eat dinner, take a shower, and then get ready to go out.

Sometimes, I would download MP3s from the Internet to listen to the songs that I wanted to sing that night. About six months into my study, I brought home a karaoke machine, very affordable at $30, a portable Memorex machine. It had no video function on the machine itself, so I plugged it into my television. It had a small speaker for the audio, and RCA jacks that allowed me to connect it to my home stereo system for a more 'Hi Fi' experience. Although there are much more fancy and elaborate (and more expensive) karaoke systems out there, the Memorex has provided me with all that I need to practice singing at home (it even has a reverb function). I ordered a handful of karaoke CDs from Amazon, including discs dedicated to The Cars, Queen, one called 'Standards,' and one was a collection titled 'Super Party Songs.' I also bought some rock CDs, including 'Classic Rock,' and 'Guitar Legends.' Because my study is about the performance of karaoke in relation to identity, I also bought a hip hop CD, and a CD featuring songs by Jennifer Lopez and Selena. Sometimes, I would practice before I went out. Because my home karaoke collection is very limited, usually the practicing was to warm up my voice, not to practice a specific song that I was going to sing that night.

I actually tried very hard *not* to practice or pick songs before I went out. I felt that there was something more spontaneous, perhaps more authentic, about getting a feel for what people were singing on any given night, and then trying to pick songs that fit with the flow of the evening. Sometimes, especially if I was very intimidated by a song but I wanted to sing it anyway, I would give in to my desire not to bomb, and would look up lyrics on the Internet, or listen to my own CD collection to remember when the singing starts, or to perfect exactly how a specific hook went. Some days, I would hear a song on the radio and think 'Oh my gosh, I have to sing that song tonight.' Many times, when I was driving to Capone's I would listen to Alice Cooper's radio show. I always liked to do this because Alice Cooper plays a lot of obscure classic rock that is not played on the radio very often. This would help me to remember songs that I liked but I had not heard in a while, which always seemed refreshing for an audience listening to the third rendition of Alanis Morissette's 'You Oughta Know' on any given night.

My own musical taste is mostly 'alternative rock' from the 1980s and 1990s, but I like many different genres of music. It is lucky that my taste in music is very diverse, because there are very few alternative songs on the 'menu' at Capone's. There were a sparse number of alternative songs that were offered, including a few Cars songs, a Killers song, and a New Order song, but when I would pick those most of the people at Capone's were not familiar with these songs, and so they were not met with as much enthusiasm. Perhaps the most popular alternative rock song I sang was Nirvana's 'Smells Like Teen Spirit,' which it seems like everybody knows, regardless of age, gender, ethnicity, or class. This song was always greeted with enthusiasm by the crowd, but it was usually met with cringes from the KJs as I screamed like Kurt Cobain in the fairly small bar, a space that was not acoustically ideal for performing grunge.

Luckily, I grew up listening to my father's LP collection of 'classic rock' from the 1960s and 1970s. Thus, I began my karaoke experiences by singing songs by the Doors, such as 'Light My Fire' and 'Riders on the Storm,' songs by the Beatles such as 'Come Together' and 'Happiness is a Warm Gun,' or songs by the Eagles such as 'Desperado' and 'Peaceful Easy Feeling.' It was within the genre of classic rock that I found the most success. I think that there are several factors for this phenomenon. On the one hand, these songs are known by various generations of people who come to Capone's. Older people know these songs because they grew up listening to them. Younger people know these songs because they have been exposed to them through their parents. On the other hand, classic rock songs are also popular at karaoke establishments because of the amount of energy they typically engender, in both the singer and the audience. Because karaoke typically happens within a context of drinking alcohol, the high-energy of rock music helps to fuel the drinking, and helps to fuel the fun.

Performing Identity

This study is further informed by the work of several social theorists and anthropologists. The starting point is the theoretical models proposed by Erving Goffman in *The Presentation of Self in Everyday Life* (1959), and expanded on by Judith Butler in *Gender Trouble: Feminism and the Subversion of Identity* (1990). Both Goffman and Butler see categories of identity as constructed through performance. This book builds on Goffman's work, and expands Butler's work on gender to look at other categories of identity as well, especially ethnicity and social class.

Writing in 1959, Erving Goffman set out to change the way that people look at the formation of the 'self.' Using the theater as a metaphor, as a 'scaffolding' within which to discuss the cultural processes that oversee the formation of self, Goffman proposes the notion of 'self-as-character': 'In our society the character one performs and one's self are somewhat equated, and this self-as-character is usually seen as something housed within the body of its possessor, especially the upper parts thereof, being a nodule, somehow, in the psychobiology of personality' (Goffman 1959: 252).

Like the phenomenologists (see Edmund Husserl 1962 and Maurice Merleau-Ponty 1962), Goffman points out that, when trying to locate a specific place in our bodies where this nodule of the 'self' resides, there is no 'there' there. Instead, he suggests that the self is a 'dramaturgical effect,' created through social situations that are performed as if they were scenes in a play. In this way, 'the self is a *product* of a scene that comes off, and is not a *cause* of it' (Goffman 1959: 252, emphasis in original). Nearly twenty years later, in his playful picture book *Gender Advertisements* (1979), Goffman applies this same paradigm to the performance of gender, documenting categories of 'gender display' in commercial images. He hypothesizes, 'If gender be defined as the culturally established correlates of sex (whether in consequence of biology or learning), then gender display refers to the conventionalized portrayals of these correlates' (Goffman 1979: 1).

In 1988, Judith Butler took up the mantle that Goffman threw down. In an article first appearing in *Theatre Journal*, titled 'Performative Acts and Gender Constitution: An Essay in Phenomenology and Feminist Theory,' Butler proposes: 'Gender is in no way a stable identity or locus of agency from which various acts proceed; rather, it is an identity tenuously constituted in time – an identity instituted through a *stylized repetition of acts*' (Butler 2007: 187, emphasis in original). Butler takes Goffman's idea about the performance of self one step further. While Goffman views the self and gender as a product of the performance of a scene, Butler views the self and gender as an inherently unstable field, a 'regulatory fiction' (Butler 1990: 180), existing only within the formation of discourse.

The merits and problems of these theories have been debated at length in other venues, and this current project is not intended to document this debate. Instead, through the use of karaoke as a vehicle, I endeavor to convince the reader of the viability of the theory that gender is constructed through performance, and that other categories, such as ethnicity and economic class, are constructed in a similar way.

Early on in my research, I realized that the clearest pictures of the performance of identity that I could paint would be descriptions of the performances of karaoke themselves, and that my deepest realizations about these performances would come from the analysis of my own experiences. In the end, I often wondered how my own identity might come into play. I wondered about how the fact that I am a white, heterosexual male might influence my study. Would it influence the kinds of friends that I would meet? Would it influence the way that other people would interact with me? Would it influence the way that I perceived certain performances? By the end of the study, I realized that my membership in certain classes probably did have some influence on the way that other people saw me, and the way that I saw other people; but I always tried to do my best to break free of these restrictions. I also realized that sometimes I had to struggle to look past my own stereotypes. In the end, however, I feel like I was able to minimize the impact of these factors.

Riders on the Storm

When I first started my study, I had grand ideas of doing a set of surveys combined with recorded interviews of 200 singers at three different karaoke bars in the Denver metro region. I wanted to show, scientifically, that people perform their identities. I was hoping that I could show this statistically, by linking how people identified themselves (in terms of gender, ethnicity, and social class) and how they identified the original singers of the songs they chose to sing. I realized early on in my research, however, that the subject of identity is so vast, and is in such a state of flux, that a purely scientific, objective approach to the study of karaoke would not be possible. To further discourage my scientific approach, I found out that even if I did administer hundreds of surveys, ran the statistics, and found a correlation, my findings would not be statistically significant, because there is no possible way to draw a random sample from all of the people who sing karaoke in the United States. I also realized that studying three different bars was unnecessary, because I could find performances of gender, ethnicity, and economic class at a bar five minutes from my house.

Furthermore, when I initially began to talk to people about their karaoke performances, especially when I brought up the subject of my book and tried to explain my theories about the performance of identity, most people were not very articulate or even interested in discussing the relationships between their performances and their identities. For one thing, I did not consider it polite or appropriate to bring up questions about one's ethnicity or sexuality when I was doing research in public. Even when I observed what I considered explicit performances of gender, ethnicity, and class, the people who I talked to were usually not aware that they were performing their gender, ethnicity, or economic class. As far as I can explain the phenomenon, the inability and reluctance of people to discuss issues of identity are perhaps due to a sort of sublimation of hegemonic tendencies. Our conception of what constitutes an appropriate performance of identity (for example, the fact that women mainly sing songs made famous by women and men mainly sing songs made famous by men) has become transparent. It is a cultural norm that has been drilled into us since we were born, when the candy cigars that our father handed out at the hospital were either pink or blue.

Begrudgingly, I abandoned my plan for surveys and statistics, and I attempted to reconcile myself to the fact that my ethnography would be interpretative. In addition, my study became streamlined from three sites to one. Although I have mistrusted the so-called postmodern 'interpretive' approach to ethnography in the past, after the first several months of my study I realized that interpretation would be the closest that I would be able to come to the 'truth.' Eventually, I was able to come to terms with this approach.

The Crisis of Representation

Some of the other theorists who have significantly influenced this study, especially in terms of the methodological approach, are the anthropologist Clifford Geertz and the performance studies scholar Dwight Conquergood. In *The Interpretation of Cultures* (1973), Geertz lays the foundations for ethnographic strategies that are used today in the fields of anthropology, sociology, communication studies, ethnomusicology, as well as other emerging fields such as performance studies. In the 1991 essay 'Rethinking Ethnography: Toward a Critical Cultural Politics,' Dwight Conquergood proposes strategies to overcome problems that some critical theorists have described as 'colonial' models of ethnographic research. In this study, in addition to the more traditional method of conducting interviews, I have utilized many of the strategies proposed by Geertz and Conquergood, including participant observation, auto-ethnography, thick description, and embodied writing. Furthermore, I have attempted to integrate Goffman and Butler's dramaturgical understandings of the performance of identity into my methodology. This approach, that is, this set of methodologies that I have employed in this study, can be called 'performance ethnography.'

Conquergood identifies trends that emerged during the late 1980s and early 1990s, as social scientists started to rethink the political implications of ethnography. Among the most profound realizations was the relationship between anthropology and colonialism. For example, the traditional ethnographic model of the anthropologist going into the field recapitulates the act of colonial occupation. Ethnographers began to question the ways their very presence in the field might be influencing the results of their study, or even worse, might be causing irreparable changes to the very cultures that they were trying to preserve. Along with the concern that the ethnographic model reinscribed colonial sentiments, was the realization that ethnographic texts often presented the anthropologist as an authority figure. The ethnographer is presented as an expert because an ethnographer is 'there.' In addition, much of the authority of the ethnographer comes from the point of view of the style of writing. Traditionally, ethnography is written in the third person. That is, the author's omniscient and omnipresent voice becomes unquestioned, equivalent to the voice of God. Without 'locating' the ethnographer within the original context of the observations, prose is written as an objective truth, rather than as originating from a subjective point of view.

In this book, I employ methods that attempt to overcome problems associated with early 'colonial' ethnographies that attempted to position the ethnographer as an authority figure. If, at times, when you are reading this book and you notice that the observations are based on my own subjective experiences, it is because I do not attempt to make the reader believe otherwise. In fact, I have attempted at all times to make a point of locating myself, the subjective observer, at the center of this research. This does not mean that my observations are sacrosanct. In fact, it means the opposite. After reading about my experiences with karaoke and my interpretations, I encourage the reader to 'question authority,' to go out and, though their own experiences, find their own truths regarding the formation of identity.

Participant observation is a method in which the ethnographer actively participates in cultural activities instead of passively observing them. Instead of standing by as a passive, supposedly 'objective' observer, I threw myself into the middle of the cultural experience of singing karaoke in order to see for myself what it was like. I probably learned more from my own experiences of singing than I did from all of the performances I observed. It is one thing to watch, but one receives a much fuller understanding of the subject when one becomes the subject itself.

With auto-ethnography, the researchers write about their experiences, acknowledging and striving to overcome their own personal biases. This method confronts issues associated with traditional anthropological research: the colonial problems of 'differencing' and 'othering' members of a culture as they are put under a microscope. Auto-ethnography focuses on one's own experiences, which means that information is gathered within a positive, affirming model, rather than within a model that is adversarial from its conception. Furthermore, auto-ethnography is a strategy that attempts to overcome the problems associated with the 'authoritative' voice, replacing the unlocated, objective voice with a located, subjective voice.

Thick description focuses on describing ethnographic sites and subjects with as much detail as possible, always striving to find the way that cultural context affects the meaning of what is observed, for both ethnographer and subject. The strategy of thick description attempts to found the ethnography in the context of the performance site. The connection between performance, identity, and culture takes place at the absolute ethnographic site: the living human body.

Embodied writing is a rhetorical style that emphasizes the fact that cultural practice is embodied. The ethnographic moment takes place in a live environment on the ground level. The experience of the anthropologist in the field relies on the interactions between the physical presence of the anthropologist and the physical presence of peoples that the anthropologist is studying. When viewed in this way, the 'field' is really a 'site for performance.' Thus, the ethnography, itself a kind of performance, must be able to somehow reconstruct, record, or at least account for that original live performance that took place in the field. The ethnographic record must show us the evidence of these bodies in performance. This is why, in this study, the sections that describe the performances that I observed are written in first person and present tense. Thus, embodied writing must be evocative, attempting to bring the reader into the living moment of the same original event that the ethnographer experienced.

It is under this framework that I propose a methodology of 'performance ethnography.' This toolset of methods has been assembled in an attempt to overcome the limitations of the crisis of representation that performance studies have only just begun to recognize by placing the human body and the site of the performance at the forefront of the ethnographic study. In Goffman's model, social behavior is organized according to dramaturgical principles. The human ethnographic subject is viewed as an actor playing a character for an audience. Thus, any dramaturgical framework for ethnography should consider elements such as setting, props, costumes, lighting, and sound. In addition to these 'onstage' elements, one should consider the 'offstage' dramaturgical elements at work behind performances of everyday life, such as the figures of authority that control the power dynamics (the director) and the interest of economic factors (the producer). One could also think of the hidden, hegemonic forces that govern cultural production as theatrical conventions: unspoken, tacit agreements between actors and audience that are embedded within historical contexts. Furthermore, because identity politics are at the center of cultural production, performance ethnography should focus on performances of identity, especially related to the important categories of gender, ethnicity, and class.

To summarize, these are the organizing principles of 'performance ethnography' that I have employed in this study: (1) performance ethnography employs a 'toolset' of methodological approaches, including participant observation, auto-ethnography, thick description, and embodied writing; (2) the thick description in performance ethnography focuses on dramaturgical elements, including actors, audience, setting, costume, lighting, and sound; (3) the embodied writing in performance ethnography is written in first person and the present tense; and (4) special consideration should be given to understanding the performance of identity, especially related to gender, ethnicity, and class.

Performing Ethnography

Perhaps, like all new ethnographers, one of the first questions I had was 'What exactly does one do when performing ethnography?' As it turns out, the main method that I employed was as simple as the directions on a shampoo bottle: instead of 'wash, rinse, repeat,' the instructions are 'sit, watch, repeat.' For any new student who wants to conduct ethnography, I would tell them this: go to a public place, a single location, at a specific time of day, wait, and watch. Observe everything that goes on. Then, return to that same location on the same day and time next week, and the week after that, and so on. Pretty soon, the events that one observes begin to reveal patterns that recur every week, patterns in the people who return to the same place time after time, and patterns in the events that happen in that location week after week. In many ways, this act of observation is the equivalent of a theater critic seated in an audience observing a performance. The critic is concerned with characters, settings, plot lines, and themes. The ethnographer is concerned with these very same things. Usually, the critic takes notes, and that is what I did, too.

Consider this hypothetical situation: what if you were a police detective conducting the investigation of a murder. You have a prime suspect that you are sure committed the crime, but you do not have any hard evidence to back you up; you only have hearsay and circumstantial evidence. In a court of law, there is the concept of a 'preponderance of evidence.' According to this line of argument, a jury can convict a defendant of a crime without direct evidence, but only if the prosecutor can show that there is a preponderance of circumstantial evidence in which it becomes clear that the defendant is guilty. In this study, I attempt to prove that people perform their identities, in terms of gender, ethnicity, and class, and that performances of these categories of identity by individuals coalesce to create communities formed around these categories. Although I do not have statistical evidence to back this up, I have attempted to assemble a preponderance of evidence to convince the reader that my hypothesis is true.

Besides the challenges associated with performing qualitative rather than quantitative research, there were several other hiccups along the way. One aspect of my plan that shifted during my study was my initial choice of wanting to tape record interviews. Eventually, I changed my mind about recording the interviews when I was talking to a colleague of mine at a conference who had done similar ethnographic research. He told me that he did not record any interviews, because of the fact that the act of recording a conversation can change the way a respondent answers questions. Once the persons interviewed become aware that they are being recorded, they often become self-conscious, and will withhold information that they do not want recorded, or they might embellish information because they think that it is what the interviewer wants to hear.

The problem associated with recording interviews is the ethnographic equivalent of the 'observer effect' associated with the Heisenberg uncertainty principle. The observer effect was created to describe a problem in the field of quantum mechanics associated with measuring the position and momentum associated with particles of light. In the case of quantum mechanics, the act of observation changes the nature of the object that is being observed. In the case of ethnography, the act of observation, whether being done through a recording device or sometimes even the very presence of the anthropologist, can also change the properties of whatever is being observed.

Besides this problem associated with making sound recordings, I found that a similar phenomenon occurs in relation to taking field notes. I found out very early on, in fact during one of my first karaoke experiences while I was in the United Kingdom for an academic conference, that writing field notes in public tends to attract attention, and can actually become a hindrance to an authentic observation. I had wandered into a 1980s themed karaoke bar in a small industrial town in the central region of the UK. A waitress who observed me writing notes thought I was from 'corporate' and she thought I was there to report on how well she was doing her job. She seemed genuinely relieved when I told her about my study. If anybody asked me why I was writing things down, I would always try to explain what I was doing. For the few people whom I had engaged in a conversation that asked me about my career and my study, I would tell them that I was writing a book about karaoke and the performance of identity. If their eyes did not immediately cross in confusion, I sometimes felt like these people, who found out that I was a writer, would 'perform' for me. That is, beyond performing for the regular audience, they would begin to perform for me, the ethnographer. It seemed as if, perhaps in a bid for minor celebrity, they were auditioning to appear as a character in my book.

Therefore, in an attempt to be discreet in my study, and to try to encourage more sincere performances, I later abandoned writing field notes while in public altogether, and I would find myself taking trips to the bathroom to scribble down my notes, even when I did not need to go to the bathroom. Sometimes I would write notes sitting in my car before driving home, or write down my memories of the performances while they were still fresh in my mind, late at night or early the next morning.

During the fall of 2008, I began to compile my field notes, which had all been written in short hand on tiny 2" by 3.5" slips of paper, actually karaoke request slips. Eventually, these field notes were rewritten on 3 × 5 index cards for easy reference. Any performance of gender that I had observed was written on pink note cards, performances of ethnicity were written on orange note cards, and performances of economic class were written on green note cards. I used stickers on the cards to code performances that fit onto more than one category. Performances that did not fit in any of these categories were written on yellow note cards. As I began to make my note cards, patterns began to emerge, and I felt that I could begin to 'write up' the ethnographic sections of my study.

Although I witnessed thousands of performances, by necessity I found I could only focus on a small percentage of them in this book. In whittling down which performances I would choose to write about, I attempted to focus on those performances that most profoundly influenced my understanding of the way that identity is constructed in performances of karaoke and everyday life, as well as those that would best serve as examples to convey what I learned in this study to the reader.

Selling Desire

In the final stage of my study, during the spring of 2009, I conduct a series of one-on-one interviews with the staff of Capone's and about a dozen of the regular singers who I have come to know during the course of my study. Talking to these people gives me a much deeper appreciation of the nuances involved in the production of karaoke.

The first person that I talk to is the Wednesday night KJ, Ron. Ron is very interested to talk to me about my study. I am equally interested to find out that Ron has a Masters degree in communication studies. I tell him that it is a fortunate coincidence, since many of the people who study karaoke are from the field of communication. In addition to his insight into what it is like to be a karaoke DJ, Ron also fills me in on some of the details of the history of karaoke night at Capone's. Karaoke started there in 1992, when a couple named John and Donna ran the show. During the early 1990s, Ron became a regular singer at Capone's. Ron explains, 'There used to be thirty or forty regular singers who came every week.'

I heard about this era from some of the regulars, and this theme continues to echo throughout the interviews. Eventually, I began to think of the 1990s as the 'Golden Age' of karaoke at Capone's. There are only a handful of people left who are still around who remember karaoke in the 1990s at Capone's, but those who do talk about those years with a glow of nostalgia in their eyes. About five years ago, Ron bought all of John and Donna's equipment, including about 1000 karaoke CD+G discs, for $900 and became the Wednesday night KJ at Capone's. Now, despite a national trend that suggests that the karaoke industry in general is on an upsweep, Ron predicts that karaoke at Capone's, or at least on Wednesday nights, may be on the decline. 'I wouldn't be surprised if Wednesday night went away. If there were four, five, six weeks in a row that are dead, they might shut it down. Saturday has a built-in audience. Sometimes I struggle on Wednesday. I don't do any promotion. I used to, but I don't know whose job that is.'

While it might seem like being a KJ would be a great job, it turns out that the job is not as glamorous as it appears. For one thing, the pay is minimal. This is one of the main factors that make karaoke such an attractive alternative to live entertainment. Ron explains, 'I usually get $150 a night, but if the till doesn't break a certain amount I only get $100. Obviously I don't make a living at this.' For his main source of income, he lives off of his retirement savings. 'If this went away I'd find something else to do.' I ask Ron whether or not he thinks karaoke is good for business, and he replies, 'One time when it was dead, Nancy said to shut it down at about eleven o'clock, and the bar cleared out. She never asked me to shut it down early again.' I ask him why he thinks that people sing karaoke. A serious expression comes over his face as he thinks, and replies thoughtfully, 'If people are experiencing something in their life, if they are forlorn, they'll sing about it.'

After I interview Ron, I talk to Tom, the Saturday night KJ. Tom began running a karaoke show at another local bar in 1992. 'I used to be in a band from about 1978 to 1983. Then I got fed up. I wasn't good enough to go solo, so I became a DJ. I still got myself out there.' He motions to his equipment. 'This was my vehicle.' Tom started a mobile DJ business in upstate New York in 1983, and eventually moved his business to Colorado in 1987. He explains, 'There was only one other guy in the business then. I'd knock on doors. It was a new idea, so I had to get out there, let people know about it. The mobile DJ thing was big, especially for weddings. The first "wow" was that it was cheaper than hiring a live band. The second "wow" was that you could play any kind of music, and choose from thousands of songs. Then later some guys figured out how to make just as much as a live band would have made.'

Tom got into doing karaoke shows in addition to his regular DJ gigs in 1992. 'I heard about karaoke and I had to get into it.' He has been doing the karaoke at Capone's for about two years now. 'This is the only place where I regularly do karaoke. It's great. It's easy. I just come here and run it. I get to sing. I love to sing.' At the same time, Tom admits that running a karaoke show is not very lucrative: 'The only problem with running a karaoke show is that any idiot can do it. You have all of these young guys who come in and say they'll work for $50 less than the other guy. I'm making less money now that I made in 1992 when I started doing karaoke. I make four or five times as much for a wedding, where I'll get $800.' Consequently, not only is hiring a KJ cheaper than hiring a live band, it is also cheaper than hiring a live DJ. (As a side note, if you ever find yourself at a karaoke bar and are in a hurry to sing, it never hurts to tip the KJ!).

Another staff member at Capone's that I am anxious to interview is Anna, who has been the lead waitress since about the time that I began singing during the summer of 2007. I am especially interested in hearing what Anna has to say because in addition to waiting on tables, she also performs karaoke on a regular basis. She is an exceptionally good singer, and I want to know how she learned to sing. She explains, 'I've been singing since I was twenty-one, about four years ago. I was trained vocally in high school. A choir teacher picked me out as a good singer, a soloist, and gave me extra lessons in singing.' I ask her about how she first got involved with performing karaoke and she answers, 'The first time I tried karaoke I bombed. It was at a place where I was bartending. Afterward I thought, "I suck, but I love this." There's this addictive thing about singing karaoke. Later I got better. A lot of it was learning how the words come up on the screen, the "oos" and the "ahs" and what to do with that.' I ask her what kind of music she likes to sing the most. 'I'm a rock girl, but I don't sing rock songs. I sing songs that I can sing: anything by Journey, "Son of a Preacher Man," or "Total Eclipse of the Heart."' I ask Anna's opinion as to whether or not she thinks karaoke is a passing fad. Emphatically, she answers, 'Karaoke is good for business. I think it's here to stay. It's not a fad.'

The final staff member that I talk to is Nancy, the bartender and general manager of Capone's. Nancy finds time to talk to me on a cigarette break. We sit down at an outside table, even though it is winter and dark outside. I ask, 'Do you think karaoke is good for business?' She says, 'Yes and no. It can be. I think without karaoke on Wednesday night we wouldn't do as well. That's why we started karaoke on Saturday nights. We used to have live music on Fridays and Saturdays, the same band both nights. But people started to come on Friday but not on Saturday.' I ask Nancy when karaoke is bad for business and she explains, 'It can be bad for business if there are two or three terrible singers, especially at the bar. Sometimes I'll hear someone at the bar say, "That's enough, I'm out of here" and they leave. So it's a balance.'

When I ask Nancy if she has any good karaoke stories, she thinks for a moment then gets a bright glow on her face. She asks me, 'How long have you lived around here?' I answer since 1992. 'Then you know who Joey Maroni is, you know the owner of the restaurant Maroni's? Well, he used to come here and sing karaoke every week. He was an institution. Everybody knew him. He even had his own table. He sang karaoke here until they came and took him away to a nursing home. He died a year after that. That was about five years ago.' Suddenly it hits me that the death of Joey Maroni coincided with the end of the Golden Age of karaoke at Capone's. I wonder if this was a coincidence.

Nancy explains to me, 'Karaoke popularity comes in waves. It's kind of stagnant right now. Maybe it's becoming more popular with young people – with the rock.' I ask her what her favorite style of music is and she says, 'Rock and Roll. I like it when people sing rock because it increases the amount of energy in the bar. More people know it, whether they are young or old. My kids know all the words to classic rock songs.' This comment comes as a sort of revelation to me. Classic rock taps into an inter-generational phenomenon, a sense of commonality and communion that is passed on to children as they grow up listening to their parent's music. Nancy tries to further explain, 'I want more energy. More energy means more people are drinking. People want to go out, have a fun time and drink.'

I suddenly understand the connection between the performance of karaoke, identity, and community. People love to sing karaoke because it satisfies their desires on several levels. On the one hand, the performance of music taps into the human desire to be understood and recognized as an individual. On the other hand, it also taps into the human desire to celebrate and be part of a community. It is at the confluence of these two desires that karaoke finds its power, a power that is harnessed by the producers of culture. In a way, the power of performance, the manifestation of presence, is the central driving engine of the apparatus of commerce. Performance is the present, embodied manifestation of power. In public spaces, when performance is happening, especially in a heightened, celebratory context, an exchange of goods is certain to be happening nearby, and feeding on the same emotions and desires that are brought to the surface by these performances.

Chapter 2

Turning Japanese

Everyone around me is a total stranger.
Everyone avoids me like a cyclone ranger, everyone.

– The Vapors

I first became interested in the idea of writing an ethnography about karaoke in 2004, when I was pursuing an interest in Asian performance styles as part of my Ph.D. studies at the University of Colorado. One of the books I read was Anne Allison's ethnography *Nightwork: Sexuality, Pleasure, and Corporate Masculinity in a Tokyo Hostess Club* (1994). This book is a fascinating study of the *mizu shōbai* (literally 'water trade') district of Tokyo, Japan, the 'red light' district where one can find a variety of entertainment establishments, many of which are connected to the sex trade. Sometimes, karaoke is one of the activities performed at these venues. Allison became a 'hostess' in one of the nightclubs where wealthy, male, Japanese businessmen are entertained after work. Allison's study is about how these hostesses help the men who frequent these bars to define their masculinity. Allison explains that the job of the hostess is not necessarily to perform sexual acts, as it is in some other kinds of karaoke establishments across Asia, but the lighting of cigarettes, pouring of drinks, and the conversation that these hostesses provide to prop up the ego of the male patrons, and, in a way, help them to 'construct' their masculinity. This collision between the construction of gendered, economic, and cultural identities fascinated me.

Another book that has been very influential on my thinking about this subject is Dorinne Kondo's ethnography of a Japanese confectionary, *Crafting Selves: Power, Gender, and Discourses of Identity in a Japanese Workplace* (1990). In this book, Kondo explains that when she began her study, she chose to work in a candy factory because it was a 'blue-collar' business, very different from the 'white-collar' Japanese businesses that have become a stereotype in American thinking. Kondo had vague notions that her study would be related to economics and kinship; but when she got into the field, something very different happened. She explains, 'It had been twenty-six months since I first arrived, and the problematic of kinship and economics had come to pivot around precisely what I perceived to be even more basic cultural assumptions: how *selfhood* is constructed in the arenas of company and family' (Kondo 1990: 9, emphasis in original). Kondo goes on to describe her own experience related to selfhood when she had a psychological episode, brought on by acclimating to Japanese society, and in particular by having problems assuming the many different roles that were demanded of her. These included roles that she was expected to play within the family she was staying with, and roles she was expected to play in the business where she worked.

Kondo explains that, in the Japanese language, there are many different pronouns for the English word 'I.' The pronoun that is used to refer to the 'self' depends on the relationship between the speakers, in terms of status. Kondo experienced a nervous breakdown, brought on by what she calls a 'fragmentation' of her 'self,' a sort of cognitive dissonance that occurred between her own cultural frame of reference, created through her upbringing in the United States, and the frame of reference she was assimilating into, that of Japanese culture. This personal episode ended up being an epiphany for Kondo, and she realized that, instead of kinship and economics, what she wanted to write about was the difference between the so-called 'western' conception of self and the 'Japanese' conception of self. Kondo explains, in most Euro-American cultures, the 'self' is assumed to be a solid, singular entity, while in Japanese culture the 'self' is conceived to be much more fluid and can shift from context to context. She writes, 'A brief consideration of work done on "the Japanese self," in light of my particular experiences in the factory and the neighborhood, can point us toward the profound challenges such scholarship offers to seemingly incorrigible western assumptions about the primacy of "the individual" and the boundedness and fixedness of personal identity' (Kondo 1990: 26).

As I began to plan my ethnographic research on karaoke, the revelation that selfhood is constructed through cultural contexts was an epiphany to me, and the construction of 'self' in relation to performances of karaoke became the topic of my study. I was also fascinated by Kondo's assertion that 'Japanese' selfhood is constructed in relation to social context, while conceptions of selfhood in the United States assume a fixed, individual identity. In his famous essay about the Balinese cockfight, anthropologist Clifford Geertz (1973) suggests that all performances contain a 'deep structure' of the culture that created them. Just as every element of a hologram contains the entire hologram, each performance contains the deep structure of that culture. Given Kondo's conception of Japanese selfhood, combined with Geertz' understanding of deep structure, I wondered if there might be differences in the way that people in each culture sing karaoke. Are karaoke performances by people in the United States more focused on the individual, while performances by people in Japan are more focused on the community? I would later find out that this hypothesis is not true, but that is where I began my study.

Kondo's story also resonated with me beyond this intellectual level. Like the breakdown of 'self' that Kondo went through during her ethnographic research, I was experiencing a personal reckoning of my own. As I was winding down my Ph.D. classwork and beginning plans for my dissertation research, I was not happy with my life. A few years earlier, I had married a woman whom I had met in graduate school, but our marriage was not in good shape, and was crumbling before my eyes. Seeing several members of my family deal with health issues, including heart disease, mental health, and cancer, and realizing that I had probably inherited the same genetic dispositions, I was approaching middle age and beginning to come to terms with my own mortality. I was having health issues. I was overweight. I was depressed. I did not realize it at the time, but I was on the cusp of a major life change. In the next few years, during the same time frame as my research unfolded,

I would go through a divorce, sell my house, and strike out on my own. By some happy accident, performing karaoke would become my saving grace.

Us/Not Us

To understand some of the possible pitfalls in undertaking a comparative study of the place of karaoke within Japanese and American culture, I turn to the anthropologist Clifford Geertz and his book *Works and Lives: The Anthropologist as Author* (1988). In the book, Geertz critiques the writing of some of the most prominent authors in the field of anthropology, including Claude Lévi-Strauss, E. E. Evans-Pritchard, and Bronislaw Malinowski. In a chapter called 'Us/Not Us: Benedict's Travels,' Geertz deconstructs Ruth Benedict's *The Chrysanthemum and the Sword: Patterns of Japanese Culture* (1946), one of the first ethnographies about Japanese culture to be written in the English language. This study was commissioned by the United States government during World War II, and advance copies were studied by military strategists who attempted to glean knowledge from Benedict's work that might help them defeat the Japanese. Thus, because it was written during the war, Benedict never actually visited Japan to perform ethnographic research. The book was written from afar.

Geertz points out that many westerners tend to write about other cultures primarily in terms of difference, especially when it comes to the culture of Japan:

> The Western Imagination, to the degree one can talk intelligibly about such a vast and elusive entity at all, has tended to construct rather different representations for itself of the otherness of others as it has come into practical contact with one or another of them. Africa, the heart of darkness: tom-toms, witchcraft, unspeakable rights. Asia, the Decaying Mansion: effete brahmins, corrupt mandarins, dissolute emirs. [...] But Japan, about the last such elsewhere located, or anyway penetrated, has been for us more absolutely otherwise. It has been the Impossible Object. An enormous something, trim, intricate, and madly busy, that, like an Escher drawing, fails to compute.
>
> (Geertz 1988: 116–117)

As Geertz points out in his ironic fashion, Benedict's writing emphasizes cultural differences between Japanese and Americans in a very 'Orientalizing' way. Perhaps difference is emphasized by Benedict because the United States was at war with Japan when she wrote the book. For example, the very first sentence of the work begins, 'The Japanese were the most alien enemy the United States had ever fought in an all-out struggle' (Benedict 1946: 1). Geertz takes issue with a particular literary trope that Benedict uses repetitively, specifically the way that she alternates between writing about a particular detail of Japanese culture and writing about the equivalent difference in American culture. Geertz calls this Benedict's 'In America/In Japan' trope. For example, Benedict contrasts eating and drinking habits, sexual habits, and attitudes toward marriage all in terms of 'Us/Not Us.' Geertz explains, 'The habit of contrasting "as-we-know" us with an "imagine that" them is here carried to climax; as though American Indians and Melanesians had been but warm-ups for the *really* different' (Geertz 1988: 117, emphasis in original).

Interestingly, the scholarly literature about karaoke is filled with similar tropes. Nearly every article and book that I have read about karaoke contains at least a summary discussion, and sometimes excruciating details, about the cultural differences between karaoke in Japan and that in the United States. 'Orientalism' is a term coined by critical theorist Edward Said (1979) to describe stereotypes directed toward people of Asian and Middle Eastern heritage. Orientalist stereotypes emphasize 'difference,' making a binary comparison between the so-called 'Oriental' and 'Occidental' cultures, dividing the world into 'East' and 'West.' These negative stereotypes are frequently 'exoticized,' positioning the 'other' as foreign or strange. In addition, these stereotypes often include a feminization of males, as well as a sexualization and infantilization of females. Orientalist sentiments ignore the fact that there are vast cultural differences between the various distinct cultures of Asia and the Middle East. While it is very easy to fall into the trap of focusing on difference in any cross-cultural study, in this book I have made every attempt to avoid the pitfalls of Orientalism.

Another dilemma is that while it is very easy to make overly broad generalizations about cultural differences, it is just as much of an error to assume that cultural difference does not exist. It is actually quite naïve and ethnocentric to gloss over the fact that people from two different cultures may hold two very different views of the world. This was one of the reasons that the field of anthropology was founded in the first place, as an attempt to understand, explain, and validate the wide variety of belief systems and cultural practices that exist in different parts of the world. Thus, when approaching the subject of ethnicity, and making comparisons between different cultures, such as America and Japan, one must wear kid gloves to not overly generalize the differences in terms of 'otherness,' but also attempt to embrace cultural differences. Soon, one can begin to see that the practices of other cultures are not much different from their own.

The History of Public Singing in Japan

Amateur singing has a long history in Japan. There are ritual figures (drawings) of singers that have been dated to the Jōmon period [14,000 BC–300 BC] and Yayoi period [300 BC–AD 250]. The earliest written evidence of singing in Japan is from the seventh century. It is possible that karaoke has part of its origins in the classical *Noh* theater of Japan. In their book *Karaoke: The Global Phenomenon* (2007), Xun and Tarocco explain, 'its origin [is attributed] to the long tradition of singing and dancing in rural Japan, which dates back to ancient times, or to *Noh*, a major form of musical drama that has been performed since the fourteenth century. The emphasis on singing and dancing in a samurai's training is also thought to have contributed to the development of karaoke' (Xun and Tarocco 2007: 22).

Interestingly, karaoke may also be partially descended from *kabuki* performances. One of the most often cited cultural precursors to karaoke is the *nagashi*, or strolling musicians, who have provided the accompaniment for singers since at least the eighteenth century. *Bungo Bushi* is a musical style that developed into a school of Japanese music. This style was originally developed by a *kabuki* actor, Miyakoji Bungo-No-Jo, who began appearing on stage in Edo in 1737. According to legend, his songs about committing suicide were so powerful that young lovers attempted to emulate them, and eventually the topic of the double-suicide was banned. Another *kabuki* actor, named Tsuruga Shinnai Bushi, one of the students of the *Bungo Bushi* school of music, developed his own singing style that became simply known as *Shinnai*. Although this style originated in the *kabuki* theater, soon the style began to be copied by the *Shinnai nagashi*, strolling musicians who would play music as they walked along the streets, looking for wealthy patrons to hire them for pay.

It is perhaps fitting, then, that the style of music originally used for accompaniment of *kabuki* singers would eventually provide accompaniment for amateur singers as well. According to William H. Kelly, writing in his doctoral dissertation *Empty Orchestras: an Anthropological Analysis of Karaoke in Japan* (1997), today: '*Nagashi* are strolling musicians who travel from bar to bar in urban entertainment districts, equipped with a guitar and possibly an accordion, performing and singing *kayōkyoku* (popular songs) and sometimes providing musical accompaniment for guests who sing. Dating to the Tokugawa period [AD 1603–AD 1868], *nagashi* have been displaced by the development of karaoke-singing' (Kelly 1997: 76–77). Despite the threat that karaoke has become to their survival, *nagashi* continue to perform today in the entertainment districts of major Japanese cities.

In addition to the *nagashi*, another cultural precursor to karaoke can be seen in the *chindonya*. *Chindonya* are groups of three or more street performers who play music and wear colorful costumes while they parade through the streets of major cities in Japan. They are typically hired by businesses to advertise the openings of new markets or *pachinko* (Japanese pinball) parlors. These performers play a combination of western and traditional Japanese instruments. Their repertoire includes military marches, jazz, traditional Japanese folk music, and songs from the *kabuki* theater. These types of performances date to the mid-nineteenth century, during the first period of industrialization in Japan. In a 2003 article published in the journal *Natural History*, Ingrid Fritsch describes how this came about: 'In 1845 in Osaka, a candy salesman named Amekatsu offered his special oratorical and theatrical talents to advertise for a local variety theater. That episode is accepted as the birth of chindonya (though the term does not appear until the early twentieth century), because it is the first documented case of advertising for someone else's products in Japan' (Fritsch 2003: 48).

What is perhaps most striking about these performances, and the reason that they are connected to karaoke, is that in contemporary times the performers are often accompanied by recorded music. Charles Keil, who is regarded to have written the first scholarly article about karaoke in English (Mitsui 1998: 32), writes about this phenomenon in his 1984 article 'Music Mediated and Live in Japan' (republished in the 1994 book *Music Grooves*).

Keil describes a group of *chindonya* that he witnessed advertising the opening for a local market in Tokyo:

> The group consisted of one man dressed in an old Japanese style playing a portable rack of two small drums and a gong, another tall man in a clown costume beating a bass drum, and a woman portraying a huge-headed doll or puppet with a tambourine in hand and a cassette player, hooked up to a battery-powered megaphone, under her skirts providing the instrumental and melodic half of the street music.
>
> (Keil 1994: 252)

According to Keil, Japanese culture has many examples of what he calls 'mediated and live' musical performances, including karaoke. In another instance, Keil describes a World War II memorial service he observed, in which two elderly Japanese men sing along with recorded music played from a phonograph. Keil also describes a *bon* dancing festival where live drummers play along with a record player. In the same article, Keil describes a karaoke scene. His conclusion is that, while playing live music to a prerecorded accompaniment may seem unnatural and even distasteful to an American musician, Japanese musicians seem to be less bothered by the intrusion of technology on the live performance event. Keil explains, 'What I find striking in these instances of mediated-and-live musical performances is, first, the humanizing or, better still, the personalization of mechanical processes' (Keil 1994: 252). Thus, it seems that the performance of a combination of live and mediated music is very common in Japanese culture, and may help to explain why karaoke first originated and became popular in Japan.

In addition to these older, more traditional precursors to the development of karaoke, there are several other cultural precursors that have only come about within the last century. During the 1920s, a brooding, emotional style of music known as *enka* developed in Japan. Interestingly, the popularity of *enka* songs was later revived during the karaoke explosion of the 1970s. Mitsui explains, 'The despairing sadness and self-sacrificing fatalism which permeated these songs harked back, in terms of both lyrical and musical characteristics, to the extremely popular song composed in the early 1920s – "Sendō Ko'uta" [Boatman's Song], which can be seen in retrospect as the forerunner of what we might call "hardcore" *kayōkyoku*' (Mitsui 1998: 40). The impetus behind the *enka* revival in the 1970s was largely nostalgic, as many older Japanese men and women sing these songs to remember a simpler time before the war.

In the 1950s and 1960s, *utagoe kissa* ('singing voice coffee shops') became popular, especially with college students. These coffee shops sprang up in conjunction with the communist movement in Japan. Although it is not entirely clear, it is thought that this type of singing was imported from Russia, as the singing at these coffee shops primarily comprised Stalinist songs. Kelly explains, 'From a performance perspective, the most significant aspect of this tradition was the emphasis on group singing, which was less emphasized in other singing traditions and which is virtually non-existent in contemporary karaoke-singing' (Kelly 1997: 74).

It is very interesting that group singing, outside of the context of this particular kind of coffee shop, does not seem to be common in Japan. When I first started this study of karaoke, I expected to find that karaoke singing in America would be much more focused on the individual, and karaoke in Japan would be focused much more on the group. In an article in Thomas Gonda's *Karaoke: The Bible* (1993), Anneli Rufus expresses the same kind of puzzlement about how karaoke singing fits in with Japanese culture: 'I keep wondering what aberration, what loophole in Japanese culture allowed for the invention and popularity of karaoke. Karaoke's masturbatory bravado seems just right for Americans, but Japanese balk at egotism' (Rufus 1993: 21). In fact, karaoke in Japan, although certainly less focused on 'celebrity' than karaoke in the United States, seems to be one of the cases in Japanese culture where the individual stands apart from the group, exploring and asserting his or her own identity.

Perhaps the most immediate cultural precursor to the invention of karaoke is the piano bar. Piano bars in Japan seem to be an idea imported from American piano bars, where patrons surround the piano player and sing along to the accompaniment of the pianist. These kinds of bars were especially popular in the United States from the 1920s onward (Gonda 1993: 37). In Japan, the manager of the piano bar, the *mastaa-san*, provides musical accompaniment for patrons who want to sing on an individual basis. Kelly describes the scene at a piano bar called 'My Way' that he visited in Japan in the late 1980s:

> The proprietor of 'My Way' played both the piano, trumpet and what looked like a variety of french horn, sometimes accompanying himself on the piano with the left hand, while playing one of the horns with his right. From the viewpoint of someone who is not musical, he appeared to be exceedingly so, able not only to play a large repertoire of songs on request and to improvise those with which he was less familiar, but also to adjust his playing to suit the particular singer he was accompanying, occasionally going so far as to gloss over a singer's particular weaknesses, which I was told by several customers, was the sign of a talented accompanist.
>
> (Kelly 1997: 74–75)

Gonda points out that in some bars, an entire band was used to accompany singers, and suggests that karaoke was a natural outgrowth of this format: 'This is especially true for Japanese popular music, it sometimes needs much more instrumentation than the typical American rock band' (Gonda 1993: 36). Thus, as Kelly points out, it is probable that bar owners turned to prerecorded accompaniment for customers as a labor and cost-saving measure (Kelly 1997: 75).

Mitsui details several examples that support this hypothesis. He explains that the first time that prerecorded music was employed in this fashion was in 1958, when a radio show began broadcasting background music, similar to Muzak, invented in the United States in the 1930s. This show was called *Uta-no-nai kayōkyoku* (popular Japanese music without singing), and was recorded by several bar owners and used as accompaniment for singing bar patrons. Mitsui maintains that this practice never became very popular, and soon died out: 'The customers were not very eager to sing, however, because the performance was never intended for amateur singing in its key, tempo and modulation' (Mitsui 1998: 36). Besides this, the practice was a clear violation of copyright laws, so it was only a short-lived experiment on the road to the development of karaoke.

Perhaps the most convincing example of prerecorded music used as accompaniment for amateur singers is from a bar in Takamatsu, Ishikawa, during the mid-1960s, where the owner of the bar hired a pianist to record songs on a reel-to-reel tape to be used as accompaniment for bar patrons. Not only did this nightclub owner contribute to the development of karaoke by providing prerecorded musical accompaniment, he also provided singers with readily available lyrics to each song. Mitsui explains, 'The owner attempted to photograph lyrics on slides and project them on a screen. Thus he anticipated karaoke singing with its ubiquitous written lyrics' (Mitsui 1998: 35). It was in one of these nightclubs, within the context of this history of public singing in Japan, where the first karaoke machine was born.

The History of Karaoke

The word 'karaoke' means, literally translated, 'empty orchestra.' Anthropologist William H. Kelly explains, 'A contraction of *kara* (empty) and *oke*, a shortened form of "orchestra" (rendered *okesutora* in katakana)' (Kelly 1997: 1). The term first came into use to describe music recordings, created without the vocals to be used in rehearsal by professional singers. These recordings were the equivalent of 'Music Minus One' tapes that were originally developed in the 1950s in the United States and later exported to Japan. Tōru Mitsui explains in his article, 'The Genesis of Karaoke: How the Combination of Technology and Music Evolved': 'The word karaoke, which preceded the advent of karaoke as we know it now and which came into use after the emergence of tape-recording, was a term used in the music industry, denoting an instrumental performance of a song recorded on a reel-to-reel tape by the house orchestra of a recording company as an accompaniment to singers' (Mitsui 1998: 40).

It was only later that the same word would be used to describe sing-along equipment that evolved during the late 1960s and early 1970s. Is was not until 1976 that Clarion, a Japanese electronics firm, used the term 'karaoke' to describe this kind of equipment. Because it is a literal translation, Mitsui suggests that the term 'empty orchestra' is misleading, and is better translated as 'the orchestra on the recording is void of vocals' (Mitsui 1998: 40). Another translation is the one suggested by Thomas Gonda, who prefers to translate the word 'karaoke' as: 'no man band' (Gonda 1993: 35).

There is some disagreement about exactly when the history of karaoke begins. Kelly explains, 'Contemporary constructions of karaoke's history [...] are invariably concerned with identifying the first authentic karaoke system. [...] This is generally accomplished by defining what exactly constitutes karaoke and then christening the earliest system which fits this definition as the first karaoke machine' (Kelly 1997: 72–73). For example, the most often cited definition for karaoke, perhaps because it was in one of the first scholarly studies of the history of karaoke, is the definition put forth by Mitsui: 'Karaoke [...] is generally understood to be commercially produced and marketed equipment, with a microphone mixer, that provides prompt selection of pre-recorded instrumental accompaniment. At the same time, the term encompasses the activity of singing with this equipment' (Mitsui 1998: 33). According to this definition, the first 'authentic' karaoke machine was invented by Daisuke Inoue, a part-time drummer who began experimenting with new combinations of preexisting stereophonic equipment as a way to accompany amateur singing performances in the early 1970s.

There are other scholars who disagree with this assessment. In the book *Karaoke: Sing Along Guide to Fun & Confidence* (1997), karaoke instructor Scott Shirai credits the invention of karaoke to Kisaburo Takagi, the president of Nikkodo, one of the first Japanese companies to manufacture karaoke machines. Shirai writes that Takagi 'personally assembled about a dozen 8-track tape players with amplifiers and microphones. He then hired musicians from a nearby cabaret to play the accompaniments' (Shirai 1997: 25–26). However, Takagi's experimentation occurred in 1978, six years after Inoue built the prototype of his first karaoke machine.

Kelly argues that karaoke is an invention with multiple inventors. Kelly argues, 'Several karaoke-like sing-along systems were developed independently of one another within the space of a five year period, each the product of adaptations and innovations to existing technologies or their recombination into new forms' (Kelly 1997: 72). Thus, while Mitsui considers Inoue to be the inventor of the first karaoke machine, Kelly argues that the evolution of karaoke happened in fits and starts rather than in leaps and bounds.

Prototypes of Karaoke

Although Daisuke Inoue is largely considered to be the 'inventor' of karaoke, there are actually several inventions of the late 1960s and early 1970s that could be considered, if not arguably contenders for the title of the first karaoke machine, 'prototypes' of the first karaoke machine. One of the first experiments that began to look substantially like a karaoke machine took place in the late 1960s, funded by a record store in Kanazawa, Ishikawa called Yamachiku. Since 1967, this record store had been producing 'Music Minus One' recordings (instrumental music with no vocal track) in cooperation with Japan Victor for the use of professional singers. These recordings were used as accompaniment for amateur singers in nightclubs. Typically, these clubs already owned jukeboxes manufactured by Victor, and Yamachiku retrofitted these machines with a microphone. The disadvantage was that these machines only provided a limited number of songs; they were rather bulky and did not last very long, because these machines employed vinyl LP records and not tapes.

In 1968, a similar experiment was undertaken by Iwao Hamazaki in conjunction with Teikoku Denpa Company, which would later become Clarion. Hamazaki began to experiment with miniature jukeboxes by combining 8-track technology with car stereos, creating the 'Mini-Juke.' The advantage was that these small jukeboxes could be placed in Japanese bars, where floor space is a premium, occupying less room than a traditional, American-made jukebox. Mitsui explains,

> When Iwao Hamazaki, who was to become a karaoke manufacturer, produced the combination of juke-box and loop cartridge, naming it a 'Mini-Juke,' he also installed a microphone and a coin-timer so that bar customers could pay and sing along with recordings. [...] The first thirty 'Mini-Jukes,' dubbed 'sing-along jukes,' were loaded with a dozen pre-recorded 8-track loop cartridges named 'music packs' and were rented out to bars.
>
> (Mitsui 1998: 36–37)

According to Mitsui's definition, this machine does not qualify as the first karaoke machine because the music recorded on the tapes was regular *kayōkyoku* music, with vocals and all, and singers would have to sing over the original vocal track.

The Invention of Karaoke

Daisuke Inoue was born on May 10, 1940, in Osaka, Japan, and brought up in the area where he lives now, Nishinomiya. While in high school, Inoue began playing the drums and began making money playing in a 'Hawaiian band that played the old dance-halls left behind by American G.I.s' (Iyer 1999: n.p.). After high school, Inoue became a bar musician, and became accustomed to playing live musical accompaniment for the bar's patrons, who often paid musicians to play while they sang. Apparently, some of the customers were such bad singers that Inoue and his band-mates developed a 'slow, follow-along style' (Iyer 1999: n.p.), which would later earn Inoue the nickname 'the "Human Karaoke Machine"' (Xun and Tarocco 2007: 20). In a television interview in 2003 on *The Adam and Joe Show*, a sophomoric comedy show produced by the British Broadcasting Company, Inoue explained, 'Well, originally I was a musician. In Kobe, there were many musicians who played background music for customers. That was a tough business though, so I invented the karaoke machine to work instead of me' (Inoue qtd. in Buxton and Cornish 2003).

In 1970, Inoue and several of his friends, who were also musicians, took over the management of a Japanese company called Music Crescent (later shortened to Crescent). In 1971, one of Inoue's bar patrons was going on a vacation with several of his employees, and he wanted to entertain them with his singing. Inoue elaborated in an interview with *Time* magazine, 'Out of 108 club musicians in Kobe, I was the worst! And the clients in my club were the worst singers!' (Inoue qtd. in Iyer 1999: n.p.). This particular businessman was such a bad singer that, to account for his singing style, Inoue recorded the tape off-tempo. He would later explain, 'That guy was worse than your typical bad singer. He couldn't hit the notes, couldn't even hold a beat. So I purposely recorded the song off-beat. And you know what? He was very happy with the results!' (Xun and Tarocco 2007: 20).

With the germ of an idea, Inoue began experimenting with the combination of a microphone mixer, a car stereo, a modified 8-track tape, and a miniature jukebox. According to Mitsui, the crowning achievement of the invention of the first karaoke machine was achieved in 1972 with the invention of a machine that is a curious descendent of an American invention, the jukebox. Mitsui explains how the prototype was dubbed the '8 Juke' and was later mass produced and marketed with the name 'Crescent Juke':

> Inoue and his colleagues recorded on 8-track tapes their own musical performances without vocals as accompaniment for amateur singers and manufactured ten tape-jukeboxes for those recorded tapes. Significantly, these were the first carefully arranged commercial accompaniment tapes for amateur singers, and they were made possible by the producers' musical background. Even more important was the fact that Inoue managed to devise instantaneous song selection by modifying the 8-track loop tape for car stereos. [...] Inoue shortened the tape loop [...] so that each pair of tracks contained just one song.
>
> (Mitsui 1998: 38)

In 1999, *Time* magazine published an article by Pico Iyer called, 'Daisuke Inoue, The Karaoke King.' The piece was part of a retrospective series looking back at the 1900s, and named Inoue as one of the 'Most Influential Asians of the Century.' The article declared Inoue 'the genius who gave voice to the common man in the 20th century' (Iyer 1999: n.p.), and lauds him as the person who is responsible for bringing democracy to people all over Asia. Iyer argues, 'The premise of "sing-along" music has always been egalitarian: if the boss can make like Paul McCartney, so can I. In the often hierarchical cultures of East Asia, therefore, it has served as [an] instrument of homemade democracy' (Iyer 1999: n.p.). Inoue is depicted as a humble and quixotic man who is part dreamer and part failed entrepreneur. 'Yet this Eastern Walter Mitty has, in his unobtrusive way, helped to liberate legions of the once unvoiced: as much as Mao Zedong or Mohandas Gandhi changed Asian days, Inoue transformed its nights' (Iyer 1999: n.p.).

Inevitably, interviews with Inoue turn to the question of why he never made a penny from karaoke, other than a copyright on plastic covered songbooks and from his current company that sells poison to keep cockroaches from infesting karaoke machines. 'Cockroaches get inside machines, build nests, and chew on the wires... this is the reason why more than 80 per cent of the machines break down' (Inoue qtd. in Xun and Tarocco 2007: 21). Luckily, Inoue has a very good sense of humor, and seems to downplay the failure to patent his invention.

In fact, Inoue says that he does not even consider himself an inventor. In a later interview with David McNeill of the British *Independent* newspaper, Inoue muses, 'I'm not an inventor. I simply put things that already exist together, which is completely different. I took a car stereo, a coin box and a small amp to make the karaoke. Who would even consider patenting something like that?' (Inoue qtd. in McNeill 2007: n.p.). Instead, Inoue likes to focus on the positive impact that karaoke has had on the world:

> As something that improves the mood, and helps people who hate each other lighten up, it has had a huge impact, especially in Japan. Japanese people are shy, but at weddings and company get-togethers, the karaoke comes out and people drink a little and relax. [...] It's used for treating depression and loneliness. Go to old people's homes and hospitals around the country and there is a karaoke machine. [...] It makes people happy. When I see the happy faces of people singing karaoke, I'm delighted.
>
> (Inoue qtd. in McNeill 2007: n.p.)

In 2004, Daisuke Inoue was awarded the Ig Nobel Peace Prize 'for inventing karaoke, thereby providing an entirely new way for people to tolerate each other' (n.a. 2004). The prize is given for achievements that 'celebrate the unusual' and 'honor the imaginative' (n.a. 2004). It is 'a joke award presented by real Nobel winners' (McNeill 2007: n.p.). When accepting the award, Inoue attempted to sing the Coca-Cola jingle 'I'd Like to Teach the World to Sing,' and the Nobel laureates responded (or rather retaliated) with Andy Williams' 'Can't Take My Eyes Off You.'

The latest moment of fame for Inoue came in 2006 when a feature film was made about him in Japan, titled simply *Karaoke*. With his usual humility and good-natured humor, Inoue takes all of this in stride: 'At least they got someone tall to play me' (Inoue qtd. in McNeill 2007: n.p.). His friend Scott Field attended the movie with him and afterward Inoue was satisfied, exclaiming: 'I get letters and e-mails from all over the world and now they've made a movie of my life story. You can't buy things like that' (Inoue qtd. in McNeill 2007: n.p.).

The Development of Karaoke

Like most inventions, the initial development of karaoke was followed by many subsequent improvements. Many of these were improvements in the technology, while other developments were purely cultural changes in the way that karaoke is performed in various parts of the world. Other changes occurred because of the way that karaoke was commercialized and marketed. After the invention of the '8 Juke' in 1972, there were several problems with the invention that needed addressing. For example, the early prototype used an 8-track tape. In order to obtain a stereo recording, two tracks were used for each song, which meant that each tape could only contain four songs. Mitsui explains, 'In the year after the appearance of this prototype of karaoke, the Crescent people entered into cooperation with T & M, a newly formed karaoke manufacturer, and doubled the number of songs recorded on one 8-track loop tape' (Mitsui 1998: 39). This was accomplished by recording in mono instead of stereo. Eventually, 8-track recordings would give way to cassette tapes, were later replaced by laser disc, and eventually digital recording technology would make all of these physical media obsolete.

Much of the early development of karaoke was driven by the commercialization of the technology. According to Mitsui, 'In [...] 1973, more karaoke manufacturers appeared, and soon the musical accompaniments recorded on tapes became much closer to original hit records' (Mitsui 1998: 39). This made karaoke more popular, because it allowed singers to emulate their favorite recording artists. Another modification to the arrangement of music was made with the addition of melodic lines to the recording, making it easier for the performer to follow along with the song. At first, the lyrics to songs were printed on paper sheets, sometimes copied by hand or photocopied. Inoue was the first to cover lyric sheets with vinyl plastic and have them bound into a book, and copyrighted this invention in 1974. Eventually, these printed sheets would be replaced by the ubiquitous video images that accompany karaoke performances.

The year 1976 marks the first time that the word 'karaoke' was used, coined by Clarion to describe their sing-along machines. During the 1970s in Japan, karaoke became popular primarily in urban bars. These nightclubs typically catered to the so-called 'salaryman' class, Japanese businessmen who derive a salary-based income working at a corporation. Thus, in the beginning, karaoke was an activity primarily performed by a very particular demographic, that of the white-collar urban male.

Technological developments were often driven by commercial interests. Many of these advances focused on trying to make the experience of singing karaoke more fun. Other advances focused on ways to make more songs available instantaneously. For example, in 1978, a component was added to many karaoke machines that would grade the singing on a scale of 1 to 100. Then, in 1980, the Toei Company changed karaoke forever with the introduction of a video component to accompany the karaoke performance, typically projected on a small television set or as a projection on a screen. This paved the way for lyrics to be displayed as a part of the video, eventually replacing the need for clumsy books of printed sheets of lyrics.

In 1982, the compact disk (CD) was invented, making it even easier to fit more songs on an even smaller laser disc. In 1983, CDs also became available in 'CD+G' format (CD with graphics), making it possible to encode video information on the same CD as the musical accompaniment. In 1985, Pioneer developed a CD auto-changer, making more songs available, and making it even easier for a commercial karaoke machine to provide instantaneous accompaniment for singers. In the same year, Pioneer introduced the first karaoke machine for home use. The push for the introduction of the karaoke machine into the home market was driven primarily by business considerations. At that time, the commercial karaoke market in bars catering to the salaryman was becoming saturated. Opening up the home market to karaoke machines was a way to capture a larger demographic, namely the two groups that had been excluded from performing karaoke previously, the demographic of women and children. The 1980s was also a significant time period in the development of karaoke because it was during this period that karaoke was exported overseas.

Another invention during this time period was the karaoke box, or 'KTV,' in 1986. A karaoke box is a small room equipped with a karaoke machine that makes it possible for small groups of individuals to perform karaoke in a private setting. Xun and Tarocco elaborate, 'The "karaoke box" [is] a fully soundproofed room equipped with state-of-the-art technology and graced with sofas and tables, where to have a drink and nibble snacks and sing in front of a big screen' (Xun and Tarocco 2007: 35). Just as the introduction of home karaoke machines expanded the market to include women and children, the invention of the karaoke box provided a similar boost. The ability to rent a small room for private performances made it possible to create karaoke establishments ('arcades') that cater to families and young people.

By 1988, the karaoke box was being marketed across Japan, and the practice had spread to other Asian countries as well. Another leap forward occurred with the development and distribution of *tsûshin* karaoke, a complex way to deliver karaoke songs digitally over phone lines. This development further increased the number of songs available for singers, and increased the speed at which they were available. In fact, the delivery of music over phone lines means that on the day a song is released, it is simultaneously made available to karaoke enthusiasts. This method of delivery was very appealing to karaoke establishments, because it meant an end to the stacks of laser discs and the need for complicated and expensive robotic disc changing systems. More recently, delivery over phone lines has been replaced by wireless delivery of songs via satellite.

Interestingly, the use of wireless delivery systems cuts out the need for a KJ, and the system is controlled directly by the singers. While wireless delivery systems are still used today in many Asian countries, in the United States the most popular form of delivery is the MP3+G, a proprietary type of computer file that compresses the data so that it is deliverable over computer networks, such as iTunes or Amazon. Typically, in the United States, KJs run their systems off a laptop computer that can hold thousands of MP3+Gs to choose from. Singers look through 'menus,' binders of loose-leaf paper that are sorted by artist and/or song title. When ready to sing, the choice of song is written on a slip of paper and handed to the KJ, who then decides which singers are called up on stage, and in what order. It is important to note that this arrangement implies a certain kind of power structure. Some KJs are infamous for calling 'regulars' up to the stage, while ignoring 'tourists' who are new to the venue.

There are many other developments in the evolution of karaoke since its invention, almost too many to mention. There is now karaoke software for personal computers, mobile devices, and Web-based applications. There are popular video games, such as *Karaoke Revolution*, *Sing Star*, *Guitar Hero*, and *Rock Band*, in which the usually passive gamer becomes interactively engaged with digital media. There are cell phones that double as karaoke machines. There are karaoke machines in cars. Some countries have karaoke as part of public transportation, with karaoke machines in taxis and on buses where all of the passengers sing along together. A recent episode of the television program *Shark Tank* featured an invention they called 'the future of karaoke,' a karaoke machine with built-in pitch correction for musically challenged singers.

Karaoke has spread to virtually every country in the world. Today, karaoke is performed in various diverse countries, including the United States; in Asian countries such as Japan, China, Korea, Thailand, Indonesia, and the Philippines; and in European countries such as Britain, Spain, France, and Italy. However, karaoke is also performed in other parts of the world where you might not expect to find it. For example, karaoke is performed in Turkey, Brazil, Russia, Mexico, Israel, and Tibet. Karaoke has been used for a variety of purposes as well. There is karaoke therapy, catering to victims of post-traumatic stress disorder. There is karaoke to entertain Navy soldiers onboard ships, and Army soldiers in the field. Karaoke is found frequently in vacation spots, in tropical resorts, and on cruise ships. Karaoke is a favorite pastime at nursing homes and is sometimes even used in church services. Karaoke is truly a global phenomenon.

Karaoke and the Movies

During the twentieth century, some of the significant cultural landmarks for karaoke occurred in the world of movies and television. After the invention of the motion picture camera in the 1880s, and the rise of the popularity of silent films in the early 1920s, the music halls died out and gave way to new forms of entertainment. Group singing was popular in the movie houses during the 1920s through to the 1940s, after live musical accompaniment was added to silent films. It was common for audiences to sing along to the live accompaniment. Thomas Gonda describes this phenomenon in his book *Karaoke: The Bible*: 'One song that was sung over and over was "By the Light of the Silvery Moon." The piano or organ would play in the orchestra pit. Words would appear on the screen and a little white ball would bounce from one word to the next' (Gonda 1993: 28). This would begin the transformation from a tradition of public singing with live accompaniment to the eventual mediatization of the accompaniment (a.k.a. karaoke).

Karaoke scenes have become ubiquitous in Hollywood movies and television, famously appearing in scenes of well-known movies, such as *My Best Friend's Wedding* (J. P. Hogan 1997) and *Lost in Translation* (S. Coppola 2003), and on popular television shows, such as *Desperate Housewives* and *Modern Family*. Beyond the more obvious connection of karaoke in the movies, there is another, more performative, connection between karaoke and cinema called 'movieoke.' Movieoke was first invented by independent filmmaker Anastasia Ariana Fite in a bar in the East Village of New York City in 2003. Soon it became popular all over the United States. Movieoke can be performed either at home or in public. The idea is similar to karaoke, but in movieoke, the participant is acting instead of singing. When performed in public, the movie is projected onto a screen behind the actor, and a separate monitor displays the words of the movie script. Fite explains on her website:

> A lot of performance styles have evolved out of Movieoke. Some people do mimicry – playing movement, voices, and timing with eerie accuracy. You don't have to know the

> movie by heart, though. Ad libbing and ensemble pieces are encouraged. If you're not comfortable performing alone, then drag up a few friends, too. In the end, as long as you give it your all, both you and the audience will love it. And beer helps.
>
> (Fite n.d.)

When performed at home the idea is essentially the same, but is of course on a smaller scale, as the movie is displayed on a television or using home theater equipment.

Karaoke and Television

Perhaps it should not be surprising that one of the very first 'Reality TV' shows was a show that appeared on Japanese television. Mitsui explains, 'Singing to a much wider public with professional accompaniment was popularized through the *Nodojiman Shirto Ongakukai* (Amateur Singing Contest), a live weekend show, which NHK, the Japanese equivalent of the BBC, started in January 1946, six months after the end of World War II' (Mitsui 1998: 39). Every show featured several contestants who would square off on each show, and the winner was announced at the end of each show. The creation of this show strangely foreshadows the invention of karaoke, and demonstrates the love that people in Japan have for amateur singing.

Amateur singing has also been popular on television in the United States. For example, the show *Sing Along With Mitch*, featuring the folksy singer Mitch Miller debuted in 1961. One segment on the show featured the famous 'bouncing ball' (appropriated from the movie halls), encouraging the at-home audience to sing along. In 1976 through 1978, *The Gong Show* featured all kinds of amateur performances, from singers to jugglers and contortionists. The fun of the show was waiting to see which performers got 'gonged' by the judges, ending their performances. From 1983 to 1995, amateur hopefuls appeared on the show *Star Search*, hosted by Ed McMahon. Today, reality TV shows such as *America's Got Talent* feature a similar variety of acts, and poor performances are 'buzzed' off the air.

1987 saw the debut of *Showtime at the Apollo*, featuring amateur singers vying to be discovered by the recording industry. The audience of the Apollo Theater in New York City has been accustomed to seeing amateur performances since 1934, and is known for being quite unforgiving of bad performances. Gonda explains how the audience at the Apollo is the opposite of a typical karaoke audience: 'I think it is the unfortunate influence of the popular television show "Amateur Night at the Apollo." The audience is most unforgiving, and booing and rejection are the rule. Talented artists and singers are regularly cut short in their performance. The Karaoke show is just the opposite' (Gonda 1993: 34). Later, *American Idol* would find a similar formula for ratings success, when audiences tune in to watch bad singers get insulted by the judges. In fact, perhaps the worst insult that can be hurled at a singer on *American Idol* is that it sounded like they were singing karaoke.

In 1990, a popular amateur singing show, *Stars in Their Eyes*, took Britain by storm. During the summer of 1992, *Karaoke Showcase* debuted in the United States, a one-hour show shown on network television. Auditions were held at shopping malls across the United States, and the best contestants were invited to appear on the show. This show was similar to the 1993 MTV show *Lip Sync*, a game show where contestants were judged on their lip-synching and dancing, and also featured a segment where the contestants actually sang.

Today, the art of singing provides for one of the most successful genres of reality television. In 2007, 37.7 million people watched the premier of *American Idol*, eclipsing all previous ratings of this show, and making the show the number one series on U.S. television. More votes were cast during the 2004 finale than were cast in that year's United States Presidential election. There is *Pop Idol* in Britain, as well as the spin-offs *Chinese Idol, Canadian Idol, Philippine Idol*, and *Australian Idol*. There is *Rock Star* and *The Next Great American Band*. There has been a new generation of singing shows, such as *The Singing Bee* and *Don't Forget the Lyrics*, where contestants are judged on their ability to remember lyrics rather than their ability to sing. In addition to shows based around singing, a host of other television shows based on amateur performance have sprung up, including *The Voice, The X-Factor, America's Got Talent, So You Think You Can Dance*, and *Dancing With the Stars*, just to name a few. Why is the contemporary public so fascinated with amateur performance? Why is singing so popular, even among people who are not professionally trained to sing?

Big Time

The exact amount of money brought in from the economic impact of karaoke may never be known. Revenue is generated by karaoke through the sale and manufacturing of equipment, the royalties collected from performance venues and paid to artists through the American Society of Composers Authors and Publishers (ASCAP), and the sale of karaoke songs and equipment directly to consumers for home use. In addition to these tangible revenue streams, there are also many intangible economic impacts of the performance of karaoke. Examples of economic impacts that are not usually included in statistics of how much money is generated by the karaoke business include purchases of food and drinks at karaoke establishments, the value of publicity for artists and record companies whose songs are performed at karaoke bars, and the money generated from the sale of derivative technologies such as interactive video games and cell phone applications.

Estimates of karaoke revenue are often limited to particular countries such as the United States or Japan. Worldwide numbers are even more difficult to estimate.

At the very least, karaoke is a multibillion dollar industry. In Japan alone, 'In 2010, the turnover of the entire sector was in the region of 8 billion euros [10 billion US dollars]' (Gaulène 2013: n.p.). *The China Daily*, a government-sponsored newspaper, reported in 2004: 'The karaoke industry in China is so strong and gigantic that in fact it has turned out to be the largest entertainment industry in China, generating multi-billions of US dollars revenue on a yearly basis' (n.a. 2004: 5). Although the karaoke industry got off to a late start in the United States, the past few years have seen even more money generated from karaoke-related businesses.

With the recent downturn in the global economy, one might predict that the karaoke business would be on the decline as well, but karaoke may be a recession-proof business. A recent UK karaoke industry press release titled 'Karaoke Booms As Recession Bites' reported that karaoke royalties paid to songwriters experienced 'a 10% increase in revenue collected from bars in the past five years, and Christmas 2008 is set to be big as workers search for cheaper parties' (n.a. 2008: n.p.). Karaoke may be on the rise as bars and restaurants across the country struggle to make ends meet. Although it is troubling to think about, in hard economic times the hiring of live musicians is often one of the first expenses to be cut. With the ability of karaoke to virtually replace the live musician, many business owners may be looking to karaoke as the cheaper alternative versus hiring live musicians.

The first decade of the new millennium has seen a resurgence in the popularity of karaoke in the United States. In 2004, an article appeared in the *New York Times* titled '"Sweet Caroline" Never Seemed So Good: So Uncool That It's Hip, Karaoke Enjoys a Comeback.' Beat writer Damien Cave declares:

> After three seasons of 'American Idol,' Bill Murray's sing-a-long during 'Lost in Translation' and spending 20 years as an extra in the drama of New York night life, karaoke is suddenly enjoying a second wave of popularity. Old Asian haunts are more crowded with English-speaking customers. Rentals of karaoke equipment at one leading East Coast distributor have jumped fivefold since 2001 and there is no sign of dwindling interest.
>
> (Cave 2004: 1)

Samantha Ronson, one of the karaoke enthusiasts to whom Cave speaks, explains, 'It's the farthest thing from cool and yet for some reason it is cool precisely because it's so far from cool' (Ronson qtd. in Cave 2004: 3). As of the publication of this book, karaoke shows no sign of slowing down in terms of its popularity and economic impact.

Turning Japanese

Given Dorinne Kondo's theory of 'western' selfhood versus 'Japanese' selfhood, the initial hypothesis of my study was the idea that karaoke in Japan is focused on community and karaoke in the United States is centered on the individual. However, as I began to read more about how karaoke is performed in Japan and other countries, and as I began to experience karaoke first-hand, I realized that this simple binarism would not hold out to be true.

This false hypothesis originally made sense to me, considering some of the things that I had learned about the performance of karaoke in Japan up to this point. In Anne Allison's book, she describes how when Japanese businessmen go out to sing karaoke after work, everyone from the company is expected to come and participate. It is understood that everyone will sing, regardless of skill level. There is also an unspoken pact that 'what happens at karaoke stays at karaoke.' In other words, no matter how out of hand the drunken antics may get, it is not talked about at work the next day.

On the other hand, in America, I assumed that the cultural obsession with celebrity would lead to karaoke performances centered on the individual. I imagined a world of 'karaoke idols,' amateur singers dreaming of being discovered. When I got into the field, I found that this quest for celebrity was very real, but only to a certain extent. Just as many people came to karaoke night longing for a sense of community as those longing for fame.

Likewise, I found that the dream of celebrity is also found in Japan. There are just as many opportunities for the individual to shine as there are in karaoke performed in the United States. As an example of this, consider that the song 'My Way' is one of the most popular karaoke songs in Japan, and is perhaps one of the most popular karaoke songs internationally. Johan Fornäs writes about 'My Way' in the article 'Filling Voids Along the Byway: Subjectivity, Play and Interactive Media':

> Written by Paul Anka (with François, Reyaux, and Thibault), it is particularly remembered as recorded by Frank Sinatra, but it has also been sung in quite differing versions by Elvis Presley, Sid Vicious of the Sex Pistols and the Gipsy Kings. It may fit well into a dominant stereotypical image of America in other countries, and its melody and lyrics are easy to remember and to perform. Its lyrical content, with its praise of individual freedom and courage, can be reinterpreted as a comment on the brave karaoke performer. It has therefore become something of a self-reflexive anthem for karaoke.
>
> (Fornäs 1998: 125)

Xun and Tarocco discuss this same issue in their discussion about the performance of karaoke in Japan: 'Ironically, the opportunity to be ostentatious in public explains much of karaoke's appeal. In a culture where the correct level of politeness is given prime importance and modesty is considered a virtue, karaoke provides an opportunity to give one's ego a boost. If vanity is universal, perhaps there is a real need to show off from time to time' (Xun and Tarocco 2007: 36). For these reasons, although Japanese culture seems to be more structured around the collective than the individual, such simple assumptions run the risk of bordering on Orientalism. Any binary model that attempts to pit 'The West' against 'The East' in terms of cultural difference faces this danger.

Furthermore, in my own observations of karaoke, I began to understand that karaoke in the United States is just as much about the community as it is in Japan and other parts of Asia. These suspicions were further reinforced when, in 2014, I had the opportunity to travel to Asia, and had my own experiences singing karaoke in Tokyo, Japan and Shanghai, China. An oversimplified, but often repeated conception of the difference between singing karaoke in Japan and that in the United States is that karaoke in the United States happens in public bars, while karaoke in Japan only happens among private groups in karaoke boxes. This public/private distinction might lead one to assume that people who sing in public are performing for their personal gratification, while people who sing in private groups are performing for the community.

Although I was only in Tokyo for a couple of days, in that time I witnessed many instances of people singing karaoke in public places. I saw people singing in several bars in the area of Tokyo called the Golden Gai, known for its tiny streets full of small, cozy bars. Later in the trip, we went to a karaoke bar in the Shinjuku district of Tokyo known for live musicians that accompany singers, and I sang karaoke in an open setting in front of a group of strangers (although we got to know each other better by the end of the night). In Shanghai, a friend who recently moved to the city brought us to sing at a private karaoke box. Although the evening started as a group of friends singing together in private, later in the evening we 'crashed' another karaoke box, an occurrence that our friend told us happens every time he goes out to sing. These events have led me to question anyone who tells me that there are basic cultural differences in the way that people sing karaoke in different cultures.

Just as there are many people in Japan who sing karaoke in public, in the United States many people are drawn to karaoke because of the community that it provides. The 'regulars' who come, week after week, some to sing and some to watch, get to know each other and eventually become good friends. Initially, karaoke is a way to 'break the ice.' Music becomes a mutual reference point for conversation. Because singers are also members of the audience, they depend on each other for mutual support. Even if an individual is not the best singer, they can always depend on their friends in the audience to applaud when they are done. Likewise, in Japan, one of the fastest growing ways of singing karaoke is *hitokara*, or singing karaoke alone, which began as a way to practice singing, but recently has become popular as a way to have fun on your own. Soon, my preconceived notions about 'western' performance versus 'Japanese' performance began to fade. I realized that, due to the spread of globalism, the cultural landscape of the world is evolving into a sort of hybridization, something that can no longer be represented or understood through simple binaries. Perhaps the 'Japanese' are becoming more 'American,' or perhaps 'Americans' are becoming more 'Japanese.'

Chapter 3

Boys Don't Cry

I try to laugh about it, cover it all up with lies.
I try and laugh about it, hiding the tears in my eyes.
'Cause boys don't cry.

– The Cure

The next singer is Nora, which may or may not be her real name. In any case, it is the name that she writes on the small slip of paper that she hands to the emcee. Nora is a young woman with an olive complexion, in her early thirties. She wears a tan, stylish knit hat and a scarf, designer jeans, and a candy-striped, red-and-white blouse. The KJ, Tom, is a silver-haired, bearded, middle-aged man with a ponytail. He picks up a microphone and speaks in a smooth, deep voice: 'Next up is Nora. Is Nora in the House? Nora?'

Nora takes the stage to the opening guitar arpeggio of 'Sweet Child O' Mine,' by Guns N' Roses, and confidently takes hold of the microphone. What comes out of her mouth is surprising: 'Where are those hot chicks? Where are those hot chicks that were up here dancing before? I need you to come and help me sing this song. Come on over here.' Three young women, from approximately age twenty to thirty, stand up from a table in the back (where Nora was sitting) and enter the dance floor, a small ten-by-ten space at the foot of the 'stage,' which is actually just a corner of the bar where two tables are removed to make room for karaoke equipment and singers.

Nora begins to belt out the lyrics using an aggressive, scratchy voice: 'She's got a smile that it seems to me/Reminds me of childhood memories/Where everything was as fresh as the bright blue sky.' For the most part, Nora is faithful to the original interpretation of this song, made famous by Axl Rose. One noticeable exception is that instead of the line: 'Now and then when I see her face,' she sings, 'Now and then when I see sexy girls.' Instead of: 'Her hair reminds me of a warm safe place,' she sings, 'Her hair reminds me of sexy girls.' During the guitar solo in the middle of the song, she further exemplifies the 'rock chick' persona. She motions to the dancing girls with a 'raise the roof' gesture, and then speaks over the microphone: 'This is where we do cocaine and have sex a lot and have you girls dance!' Despite the fact that Nora has been very faithful to the song in musical terms, she has subverted the song's meaning because of the fact that the original song was made famous by a male singer. In fact, since she keeps most of the original lyrics intact, the song comes off as if she is singing about a female lover, her 'Sweet Child O' Mine.' Nora takes on an ambivalent gender role in the performance when she mimics the gestures of the masculine 'rock' persona of Axl Rose. The presence of her dancing 'groupies' further complicates landscape of gender performance.

Based on this example, a performance filled with gender bending lyrics and supported by a doting female fan base, if one were to guess the sexual orientation that Nora identifies with, one might think that Nora is a lesbian. Imagine how surprised I am when I notice Nora leaving the bar about ten minutes after she finishes her song with a good-looking young man dressed in a khaki sports jacket with matching pants and wearing gold-rimmed reading glasses. As she walks out the door, she throws her arms around him and gives him a deep kiss squarely on the lips. Perhaps this act is intended to point out her actual, normative sexuality, or perhaps it is a gesture intended to further complicate the landscape of gender performance. On this night, through the magic of karaoke, Nora has temporarily taken on the persona of the male rock star Axl Rose. Yet, apparently, this performance does not necessarily say anything about Nora's actual sexual orientation. This example demonstrates one of the many ways that karaoke can be used subversively. It shows that performances of gender do not necessarily correlate with performances of sexual preference or biological sex. Thus, performances of karaoke are revolutionary in the way that they destabilize fixed notions of identity, and open up a space for the transformation of traditional gender norms.

The Ten Commandments of Karaoke

Most karaoke performances occur in public, within a space of cultural production. Because of this, these performances can be imbued with great political power. Not surprisingly, members of dominant cultural groups sometimes attempt to make 'rules' to regulate its production. In his 1991 book *Hito-wa naze utau-noka* (Why Do Humans Sing?), Keizaburō Maruyama proposes seven 'taboos' for karaoke performance in Japan. Among these are rules about not singing when one is drunk and warnings not to hog the microphone. Number five of Maruyama's seven 'rules' of Japanese karaoke is 'Do not sing songs written for the opposite sex' (Maruyama qtd. in Mitsui 1998: 18). Tōru Mitsui writes about these rules in his introduction to the book *Karaoke Around the World: Global Technology, Local Singing* (1998). Mitsui hypothesizes, 'What purposes do these rules serve? Apparently they serve to regulate politeness in public space. The "don'ts" in Japanese karaoke are valued for maintaining social gender hierarchies. This preservation of discipline distinguishes the karaoke space from a place of unrestrained play' (Mitsui 1998: 19).

William H. Kelly discusses a similar set of rules in his 2002 article 'Training for Leisure: Karaoke and the Seriousness of Play in Japan.' In an article originally published in the Japanese gossip magazine *Josei Seben* (Women Seven), readers are given ten pieces of advice about karaoke singing, which are especially relevant to young women who go out to sing with their employers: 'The singing-with-a-friend-on-a-Saturday frame of mind is not appropriate! From basic manners to what not to sing and fashion, teaching you all the keys to avoiding blunders' (*Josei Seben* qtd. in Kelly 2002: 158–159). Xun and Tarocco call these the 'Ten Commandments' of karaoke (Xun and Tarocco 2007: 42). These 'commandments' include instructions to listen intently while your boss is singing, and warnings about avoiding singing sexy songs or wearing sexy clothes that might offend the 'senior' office ladies.

Perhaps it is not surprising that 'rules' and 'commandments' for singing karaoke exist in Japan, a society that is very concerned with social hierarchies and maintaining the social order, but I was surprised to find that similar rules seem to exist for singing karaoke in the United States. Some of these rules are embedded in the way that the karaoke software works. For example, when two people choose to sing a duet such as 'Summer Nights,' the song from the musical *Grease* made famous by John Travolta and Olivia Newton John, the words on the screen appear according to a set of gendered conventions. I first observed this phenomenon when a couple at Capone's picked 'Paradise by the Dashboard Light,' the anti-love song written by 1970s recording artist Meat Loaf. When the song begins, the words for the male part appear in blue lettering, while the words for the female part appear in pink lettering. In those sections when both parts of the duet sing together, the words appear in green lettering. Sometimes, there is also a symbol that appears in front of the words for each part, a 'spade' for the male part, and a 'heart' for the female part. According to Xun and Tarocco, these conventions for gendered singing come from the karaoke conventions of 'Cantopop,' a subgenre of Chinese popular music that originated in Hong Kong (Xun and Tarocco 2007: 112).

Sometimes, these conventions, which originated in Asia, can provide for some awkward moments in karaoke performances in the United States. Once, I observed two women who got up to sing 'I Got You Babe,' the song written by Sonny Bono and made famous by Sonny and his wife at the time, Cher. Clearly, the two women had not entirely thought out the implications of the song that they had chosen. When the words began to appear in blue and pink lettering, there appeared to be a sense of confusion between the two women as to which of them should sing the 'male' part and which of them should sing the 'female' part. Apparently, they both seemed a bit taken aback by the framing of their relationship that had inadvertently occurred due to the conventions of the karaoke machine. This event provides an example of how codes of gender performance can become reified by technology. Furthermore, it gives us insight into one of the many ways karaoke performance and gender performance intersect.

Women's Songs

In *Karaoke Nights: An Ethnographic Rhapsody* (2001), Robert Drew discusses a game that is frequently played at karaoke establishments called 'karaoke roulette.' This game can be played in a variety of ways. Sometimes songs are randomly drawn out of a hat, while other times the Karaoke Jockey picks the song for each performer. In the case of Drew's example, as each contestant in the game approaches the stage, the KJ asks people from the audience to shout out random numbers and letters, and then these random codes are punched into the karaoke machine. The effect is that each participant is forced to sing whatever song comes up, which provides for some interesting combinations of performers and songs. Drew observes how karaoke roulette differs from traditional karaoke, and how this game relates to the play of identity that karaoke provides, especially in terms of gender identity. Drew explains:

> When you're in the thick of a game of karaoke roulette, your potential for identity play seems limitless. Yet in standard karaoke, where you choose your own songs, you tend to tread more lightly. You find that social pressures come to bear on you in the form of 'person-role formulas,' expectations about who may act in what capacity. In choosing a song, you can't help being mindful of the agreement between the original artist's demographics and your own, if only because others seem so mindful of it. Gender categories, in particular, are habitually invoked by fellow performers and emcees: 'You can't do that, that's a woman's song!'
>
> (Drew 2001: 59–60)

The existence of 'women's songs' and 'men's songs' in karaoke culture shows how, just like in everyday life, gender norms can put strict limitations on behavior. In addition, it is a clue about how these norms come about. In the example of karaoke roulette, there is a temporary relaxing of what seem to be the 'rules' of gendered behavior in karaoke performance. Furthermore, these rules are enforced by our peers (other singers) and by authority figures (the KJ).

Drew introduces us to Wayne, who provides an example of what can happen when a person defies these expectations. Wayne is a very good singer, but he often chooses to sing so-called 'women's songs,' such as 'Over the Rainbow,' by Harold Arlen and E. Y. Harburg, made popular by Judy Garland. Although many people in the audience love to hear Wayne sing, because he has a beautiful voice, others in the audience are not so tolerant. Drew explains the jokes that people often make at Wayne's expense. One man in the audience, Jim, calls Wayne 'Twinkle Toes.' He jeers at Wayne's performance: '"Watch his toes," Jim says, as Wayne now and then rises to the balls of his feet. Jim watches in silence for a while. "This guy sings very good," he says. "Some of the songs he sings are very quifty."' Drew asks, 'Very what?' Jim answers, 'Quifty […] like faggoty' (Drew 2001: 66). Jim's homophobic reaction to Wayne's singing demonstrates that when rules of gender behavior are broken, people's reactions can be quite hateful.

Cindy, one of the karaoke singers that I conduct an interview with, tells me about a similar story with a better ending. She recounts, 'At one place in Denver there's this gay guy who sings Whitney Houston's "I will always love you." At first, people are like, "Oh my God he's so gay." Then after they hear him sing they are like, "Oh my God he can sing," and they applaud him.' Although eventually the crowd accepted Cindy's friend because of his great voice, the gender taboo was still in play.

Drew explains that sometimes he likes to sing 'women's songs,' just to see how other people will react. He explains, 'For my own performances, I often choose female vocals – partly because some of my favorite songs are female vocals, but also in order to gauge reactions.

Emcees sometimes greet these requests with gentle provisos such as "That's a little high for you" or "Isn't that a woman's song?"' (Drew 2001: 103). On the rare occasion that men do choose to sing women's songs, they often adopt a mocking performance style that calls attention to the fact that they are performing the song as a joke. Drew muses, 'I've seen men do women's songs in karaoke bars before – men doing Patsy Cline's "Crazy" ludicrously off-key, doing Irene Cara's "Fame" in a piercing falsetto, doing Helen Reddy's "I am a Woman" in the voice of Arnold Schwarzenegger. Yet it is almost always played for laughs. [...] Female performers, on the other hand, readily do male vocals without resorting to such tricks' (Drew 2001: 65–66).

Exciting Tensions

To test Drew's theory, I decide to try to sing a 'woman's song' at Capone's. I had once seen a very interesting version of the Britney Spears song 'Baby One More Time' performed by a man on the reality television show *Rock Star*. Inspired by this performance, I download the song from iTunes, and print out the lyrics so I can practice. I want to try to sing the song as sincerely as I can. I also feel that if I am going to attempt this song then I need to do a really good job. Still, I feel more nervous than I ever have about singing.

As I turn in my slip of paper, I look for a reaction from the KJ. He is silent, but I see his eyebrows rise and his eyes get big as he reads my request. When Tom calls me up to sing, he bellows into the microphone, 'OK, Kevin is going to sing ...' he pauses and finally says, almost in the form of a question, 'Britney Spears?' As I begin the song, I realize that, despite all of my practice, my performance is not going well. Because the song is keyed at a much higher key than I am accustomed to, I attempt to lower my voice to an octave below that of Britney's key, but I struggle to hit the right notes. I also find myself making my voice rougher and tougher than usual, perhaps as a way to signal to the audience, 'Yes, I am doing a women's song, but I am a man!'

Despite what I think is a very poor performance, several of the women in the audience get up and dance along to the beat. After the song is over, the audience politely applauds, and the KJ muses, 'OK. That was ...' he utters a long pause, and finally settles on: 'interesting.' I am not surprised at all by the KJ's reaction. I am surprised, however, that the only negative feedback that I receive is from other men, not women. This suggests that the enforcement of male gender norms, at least in this case, is more often performed by other men. I am also surprised by the extent of my own internal struggle to sing the song seriously. I interpret this extreme case of nerves and my inability to sing the song without breaking frame as due to my own internalization of the discipline of gender norms, which apparently have become inscribed though the experience of my own cultural upbringing.

These experiments performed by Drew and myself point out the existence of unspoken social rules that govern the expectations that people have about the performance of identity. Furthermore, it shows that these so-called rules can be transgressed in ways that challenge people's expectations. Johan Fornäs explains in his article 'Karaoke: Subjectivity, Play and Interactive Media':

> The opportunities for transgressive interpretations are particularly interesting. Performers can opt to sing a song in a new and different way, but it is also possible to create a provocative contrast to the original only by one's choice of song, i.e., by virtue of one's social and subjective identity. For example, one might choose a song that 'fits' an age-group, sex, class, ethnicity, geography or taste that is far from one's own position. When men sing a song that is normally sung by women, the 'first-person voice' of which is conventionally perceived as female, exciting tensions may arise.
>
> (Fornäs 1994: 98)

These 'exciting tensions' created by transgressive performances point to a potential site of social anxiety. A more complete understanding of the way that these tensions come about from the transgression of cultural norms might be applied to a new way of thinking about the performance of gender.

Disruptive Divas

The previously described performance by Nora is perhaps a perfect example of how karaoke can provide a fluid, unstable field of play in which traditional gender roles can be subverted. In the book *Performing Glam Rock: Gender and Theatricality in Popular Music* (2006), Philip Auslander describes a similar performance by Suzi Quatro, the British musician of the 1970s who can be credited as the first woman of glam rock:

> Dressed in a black leather jump suit accessorized with black leather bracelets and a studded leather dog collar, surrounded by three large, hirsute male musicians in black pants and black muscle shirts, Suzi Quatro crouches at the vocal mike. Her fingers thump out notes on her bass guitar as she sneeringly shouts the seemingly nonsensical and virtually unintelligible lyrics to her first number one hit 'Can the Can.' The bass guitar is suspended low against her hips; she stomps her feet to the rhythm and thrusts her pelvis forward, against the bass, and back in a humping motion. With each cry of the lead guitar on the bridge, she thrusts herself toward the microphone with growing urgency as her vocals rise in pitch to climax finally at the chorus.
>
> (Auslander 2006: 193)

Like Nora, Quatro subverts traditional gender norms by 'crossing the line' of what is expected from male and female performers. Auslander borrows the term 'Disruptive Divas' from Lori Burns and Mélisse Lafrance (2002) to describe such performances.

According to Auslander, this performance by Quatro is typical of a style that musicologist Simon Frith colorfully calls 'cock-rock.' Frith explains what he means by 'cock-rock' in his book *Sound Effects: Youth, Leisure, and the Politics of Rock 'n' Roll*: 'Cock-rock performers are aggressive, boastful, constantly drawing audience attention to their prowess and control. [...] Lyrics are assertive and arrogant, but the exact words are less significant than the vocal styles involved, the shrill shouting and screaming' (Frith 1996: 227). Frith's discussion of cock-rock is concerned with how male sexuality is constructed in performance. According to Frith, 'Girls are structurally excluded from this rock experience: it "speaks out" the boundaries of *male* sexuality' (Frith 1996: 227, emphasis in original). Subversive performances like those of Quatro and Nora question the assertion that females are excluded from being cock-rockers. Even though they do not possess the biological 'equipment,' they are able to mobilize the same strategies to a different end. In both cases, the act of a female performer taking on the masculine persona of cock-rocker subverts traditional boundaries.

Auslander writes:

> Lafrance outlines the four conditions that have to be met for an artist to be considered a disruptive diva: she must engage in 'the creative interrogation of dominant normative systems'; create music that has an unsettling or disquieting effect on the listener; produce 'Manipulations of conventions and styles [such as] unexpected instrumental and/or vocal strategies'; and participate extensively in 'the technical and creative operations of music making.'
>
> (Burns and Lafrance qtd. in Auslander 2006: 207)

According to these criteria, both Suzi Quatro and our karaoke performer Nora qualify as Disruptive Divas.

Auslander writes about Quatro in the context of his book about glam rock, a genre of music that came about in the 1970s, led by artists such as Marc Bolan, David Bowie, and Roy Wood. According to Auslander, glam rock came about primarily as a response to another genre of music, psychedelic rock. Psychedelic rock was at the center of the counterculture movement of the late 1960s, and was typified by 'heady' interior performers such as John Lennon of the Beatles and Grace Slick of the Jefferson Airplane. One of the central idealistic tenets of this genre was 'antiocularity,' or a distrust of pure spectacle that was thought to be inauthentic, and reduce the impact of the music. Auslander quotes musicologist Lawrence Grossberg, who explains in his influential article 'The Media Economy of Rock Culture: Cinema, Post-modernity, and Authenticity': 'The authenticity of rock has always been measured by its sound. [...] The eye has always been suspect in rock culture' (Grossberg 1993: 204). This antiocularity was thought to advance the agenda of the counterculture, which linked visuality to mainstream modes of mass manipulation such as advertising and political campaigns.

Although the participants of the psychedelic rock movement wanted to challenge the establishment, there was a major contradiction at the heart of this movement that had to do with the way that gender and sexuality were constructed within this ideology. Auslander states, 'Although the counterculture professed openness about sexuality and some gay people were attracted to its centers (especially San Francisco), the counterculture's actual sexual practices were generally conventional. [...] During the 1960s, the number of prominent rock performers who were female or of color was observably very small, and no rock performer publicly claimed a homosexual identity' (Auslander 2006: 30–31). Thus, glam rock, rooted in overt theatricality instead of a kind of interior antiocularity, was a response to this contradiction.

Auslander discusses how Suzi Quatro often changes the pronouns in the lyrics of songs she covers as a way to subvert gender norms: 'In Quatro's musical performances, her body and voice, socially encoded as feminine, convey songs and gestures culturally encoded as masculine. Neither signification absorbs or negates the other; rather, they form an unstable compound – the female cock-rocker – whose internal tensions open up other possibilities for signification' (Auslander 2006: 213). One way to describe this shifting relationship is through 'female masculinity,' a phrase coined by Judith Halberstam, which Auslander explains as, 'A refusal on the part of masculine women to repress that aspect of themselves in favor of the masquerade of normative femininity' (Auslander 2006: 212).

In addition to 'female masculinity,' Auslander points out that the flip-side of the term, 'masculine femininity,' can be used to describe men who embrace their feminine side and refuse to act masculine. Auslander also explains the concept of 'butch-femme' identities, an idea that has been written about at length by feminist scholars such as Judith Butler (1990) and Sue-Ellen Case (1989). Auslander explains, 'Butler defines the butch identity as one in which "masculinity [...] is always brought into relief against a culturally intelligible 'female body.' It is precisely this dissonant juxtaposition and the sexual tension that its transgression generates that constitute the object of desire"' (Butler qtd. in Auslander 2006: 214).

In this way, gender differences can be understood as a kind of necessary evil, embedded in the politics of desire. This suggests that 'butch-femme' identities (and top-bottom identities in the world of gay men) can be understood as a consequence of human sexuality, regardless of whether that sexuality is heterosexual or homosexual. Human relationships, especially romantic relationships, are dependent on what is perhaps an innate human quality of the desire for an 'Other.' Auslander concludes, 'There is no intrinsic connection between coded displays of masculinity and femininity and the biological state of being male or female' (Auslander 2006: 140).

Auslander's observations about glam rock echo a similar argument made in Richard Dyer's 1990 article 'In Defense of Disco,' in relation to the way that the participants of the gay subculture in the 1970s turned to disco music as mechanism for social change. Dyer points out that many critics have dismissed disco as a force for cultural change outright, because they view it as more entrenched in the capitalist economic structure than rock is. The first problem with this argument is that rock is produced by the same capitalist mechanisms as disco, and it is impossible to 'produce' anything outside of these already established modes. Beyond this, Dyer argues, there is confusion between the capitalist mode of production and capitalist ideology:

> This mode of cultural production has produced a commodity, disco, that has been taken up by gays in ways that may well not have been intended by its producers. The anarchy of capitalism throws up commodities that an oppressed group can take up and use to cobble

> together its own culture. [...] It is a 'contrary' use of what the dominant culture provides, and it is important in forming gay identity, and it has subversive potential.
>
> (Dyer 1990: 413)

In a parallel way, karaoke music, although just as much a product of capitalism as rock and disco, has been taken up by contemporary countercultural elements of society as a way to rebel against traditionally held notions of fixed categories of identity. In retrospect, karaoke performances such as Nora's version of 'Sweet Child O' Mine' would not have been possible if it were not for the early pioneers of glam rock and disco. This may seem like a small achievement, but consider the hold that social conservatism had on society prior to the 1970s. These two cases of female cock-rockers, Nora and Quatro, the Disruptive Divas, are examples of how the rules of gender performance can be broken. These performances open up a space for resistance and self-reflexivity that questions the validity of the so-called 'rules' of normative gender behavior.

Performing Masculinity

Beyond demonstrating that performances of gender can be subverted, Nora's performance teaches me something else that is an important finding of this study. On the night of Nora's performance, I am called up to sing right after her. As I approach the stage, I take in what I have just seen. Apart from her banter about 'hot chicks' and random drug references, there is something else about Nora's performance that will stick with me. As the KJ pages me, 'Next up is Kevin. Let's hear it for Kevin,' butterflies rage in my stomach. The first few chords of 'Just What I Needed,' by The Cars, are pumped over the speakers, and I launch into my best Benjamin Orr impression: 'I don't mind you comin' here and wastin' all my time/'Cause when you're standin' oh so near I kinda lose my mind, yeah.' As I sing, something happens that I have never experienced before while singing karaoke.

I have never been known for my singing ability. Apart from singing in the school Christmas programs and occasionally at a church service, I have not had a lot of singing experience in my life. I have never taken a singing lesson, nor have I had any type of vocal training. In fact, I only recently started to sing in order to experience what it is like to sing karaoke from a participant observer perspective. I have had my share of karaoke failures. I have had many turns at the microphone when it felt like hardly anyone, or perhaps no one, was listening to me; or perhaps they were barely tolerating me while they nursed their drinks and waited for the next singer. Yet, tonight, something is very different. There is something in the air.

Suddenly, I feel as if the entire bar is focused on me. They are listening to me intently, captivated by my performance. Perhaps it is because Nora has warmed up the audience, or perhaps it is that subconsciously I have picked up some of Nora's 'attitude.' As the final notes of the song end, the audience erupts in applause, louder than I have ever heard for one of my performances.

There came many times after that day that I tried to emulate Nora's attitude, with varying degrees of success. Thinking back on what made that performance special, versus all of my mediocre (or worse) performances up to that point, was that I had emulated Nora's confidence and swagger. I had somehow stumbled on what it means to be a rock star. Being a star means having power – the power to captivate an audience with sheer attitude. I soon realized that the success of Nora's performance depended on an appropriation of a masculine attitude. But what exactly does that mean? Is masculinity associated with aggression, as Frith (1981) suggests? Is masculinity associated with violence, as Simone de Beauvoir (1973) writes? It is a common perception that men are more aggressive than women, and are responsible for more of the violence in the world than women are, but explaining away masculinity with these kinds of clichés is totalizing, and obscures a deeper, more complex structural formation that exists at the heart of masculinity. Ultimately, performing masculinity is more about an attitude of confidence and assertiveness than it is about aggression. This seems to contradict Frith's assertion that 'cock-rock' is about masculine aggression, or at least suggest that Frith's understanding of the connection between rock and masculinity is an oversimplification.

Ruth Padel writes about the connection between rock music and masculinity in her book *I'm a Man: Sex, Gods and Rock 'n' Roll* (2000). According to Padel, rock music and masculinity are both structured around 'beat.' Padel explains this idea in the context of a performance by American punk artist Patti Smith: 'The generation that made rock was "the beat generation." But "beat" is also the essence of male sexuality. "Male ecstasy in performance starts here," said Patti Smith in 1978, jerking an imaginary cock at her groin. "Building and building till the big spurt at the end"' (Smith qtd. in Padel 2000: 11). Padel's link between rock music, beat, and masculinity is not unlike Frith's theory of 'cock-rock.' Sometimes I wonder, however, to what degree theories like this hold true. In some instances, I feel like this kind of oversimplified interpretation of rock music as male masturbatory practice is misguided and even borders on misandry. In fact, interpretations in this vein risk reinscribing traditional gender norms, because they insinuate that it is not proper for a female to perform rock music. In my observations of karaoke, I witnessed countless women performing rock songs with the same kind of braggadocio and self-confidence as their male counterparts, using karaoke performance as a means to subvert traditional constructions of gender.

Female Machisma

The critical discourse concerned with the subject of gender in music takes place against the backdrop of a majority of critics who consider rock music, and to some extent popular music at large, a masculine domain. Historically, from the earliest stages of the rise of rock as a popular form of entertainment, men have governed its production, and the majority of the performers and consumers of rock music have been male. This has led some scholars to suggest that, in order to make a significant historical contribution, women in rock should somehow be held to a different standard than men. In the article 'Rock and Sexuality,' Frith and Angela McRobbie explain, 'Some feminists have argued that rock is now essentially a male form of expression, that for women to make nonsexist music it is necessary to use sounds, structures, and styles that cannot be heard as rock. This raises important questions about form and content, about the effect of male domination on rock's formal qualities as a mode of sexual expression' (Frith and McRobbie 1990: 372).

Simon Reynolds and Joy Press write about this subject at length in their book *The Sex Revolts: Gender, Rebellion, and Rock 'n' Roll* (1995), chronicling the history of women in rock and the 'strategies' that they have employed. Performances similar to Nora's are categorized as 'female machisma' (being 'one of the boys,' or the 'tomboy approach'), exemplified by artists such as Quatro, Joan Jett, Lita Ford, and Chrissie Hynde: a 'hard-rock, punky attitude, women impersonating the toughness, independence and irreverence of the male rebel posture' (Reynolds and Press 1995: 233). The second category is the 'feminine' approach, which 'tries to imagine a female strength that's different but equivalent' (Reynolds and Press 1995: 233), taken up by artists such as Sinead O'Connor, Suzanne Vega, Liz Phair, and Tori Amos. The third category, the 'dressing up' approach, ransacks history and mythology for provisional identities that can be used as weapons (Reynolds and Press 1995: 233–234), employed by singers such as Madonna, Siouxsie Sioux, Annie Lennox, and Grace Jones. Finally, the postmodern 'all fluxed up' approach, 'explorers of the agony and ecstasy of living with contradiction and irresolution [...] rebelling against identity itself' (Reynolds and Press 1995: 234), used by musicians such as Patti Smith, Rickie Lee Jones, Joni Mitchell, and Mary Margaret O'Hara.

Although Press and Reynolds attempt to point out the strengths of these various strategies, their analysis invariably ends with them bemoaning the failure of each approach. In the afterword of the book they conclude, 'If there's a problem with the new surge of female activity in rock, it's that innovations have remained mostly at the level of content [...] Women have seized rock 'n' roll and usurped it for their own expressive purposes, but we've yet to see a radical feminization of rock form in itself' (Reynolds and Press 1995: 387). Philip Auslander rebuts this conclusion: 'Taken as a whole, the gender critique of rock holds female rockers hostage to an historical imperative underwritten by a master narrative of progress; it is not enough for women to make rock music; they must also remake rock by transcending its masculinist origins and gendering it specifically female' (Auslander 2006: 209). Unfortunately, holding women to a kind of higher standard, a higher threshold of consideration for their contributions to the history of music than men is totalizing and, ultimately, regressive.

Performing Femininity

Sarah is a young, attractive woman in her early thirties. I have never seen her before at Capone's. She is dressed in a ribbed, low-cut, white cotton tank top, a medium-length, blue silk skirt, decorated with a pink-and-white floral pattern, white tights, and light tan strappy sandals. As she approaches the stage, she picks up the microphone and begins to sing the song 'Just a Girl,' written by Gwen Stefani and Tom Dumont of the band No Doubt. Sarah holds the microphone delicately with her thumb and three fingers, with her pinky finger dangling gently aside, and gently sways her hips from side to side.

The song 'Just a Girl' has been deemed an anthem of the 'girl power' movement. The lyrics are a gentle complaint, a tongue-in-cheek rant about the expectations that society holds over women. It begins, 'Take this pink ribbon off my eyes/I'm exposed and it's no big surprise/ Don't you think I know exactly where I stand/This world is forcing me to hold your hand.' Although Sarah's demeanor is very dainty, her voice is very strong and assertive. As she approaches the chorus, her voice rises in intensity and she sings, ''Cause I'm just a girl/I'd rather not be/'Cause they won't let me drive late at night/Oh I'm just a girl/Guess I'm some kind of freak/'Cause they all sit and stare with their eyes.' As she spouts out this last line, she makes a motion across her chest, brushing her breasts with her hand. At this point, it is not entirely clear whether Sarah is objectifying herself, or if she is playing along with the coy irony of the song. Either way, her performance is an excellent example of a performance of femininity. Furthermore, it points to the fact that it is often the male gaze that defines what behavior is considered 'feminine.' This brings us back to Butler's definition of gender as a 'stylized repetition of acts.'

Butler writes more about this idea in her book *Gender Trouble: Feminism and the Subversion of Identity* (1990). She argues that gender differentiation originated as a conflation between cultural understandings of gender behavior and biological sex. Furthermore, this confusion is rooted in the politics of desire. Butler writes:

> The institution of a compulsory and naturalized heterosexuality requires and regulates gender as a binary relation in which the masculine term is differentiated from a feminine term, and this differentiation is accomplished through the practices of heterosexual desire. The act of differentiating the two oppositional moments of the binary results in a consolidation of each term, the respective internal coherence of sex, gender, and desire.
> (Butler 1990: 30–31)

Butler's notions of gender regulation have been highly influenced by the ideas of Michel Foucault. Foucault is especially interested in how discourses surrounding gender, sex, and desire become 'naturalized' and used for the purpose of the maintenance of power (see Foucault 1977). 'Naturalization' is the process by which cultural aspects of behavior become understood to be due to biological differences.

A related concept, and a mode of thinking that can be just as dangerous as naturalization, is 'essentialism,' the idea that there is an 'essence,' or an unchanging truth associated with certain biological or cultural factors, based only on ontology. Essentialism and naturalization have historically been used as rationalizations to support the negative treatment of people of a certain gender, ethnicity, or class. Not to exaggerate, but similar reasoning lay behind the treatment of certain classes of people by Nazis in Hitler's Germany. The eugenics of the holocaust was carried out with the purpose of eliminating people with cultural traits that the perpetrators of these crimes considered undesirable. This is certainly an extreme example, but serves to demonstrate the dangers of assuming that people are a certain way because of their genetic makeup.

As an extended example, consider that in contemporary Euro-American culture, the color blue is associated with boys, and the color pink is associated with girls. Some people might assume that this color preference is a natural, essential trait based solely on the ontological fact of whether one is born a boy or a girl. When we look to other cultures of the world, however, we find that this idea about pinks and blues is not universal across cultural and historical sites. In fact, in some cultures pink is considered a masculine color, whereas blue is considered a feminine color. In the book *Pink and Blue: Telling the Girls From the Boys in America*, sartorialist Jo Barraclough Paoletti explains that the cultural association between colors and gender differences has only become prevalent in America over the last century: 'Sources from the early twentieth century prove that there was little agreement among manufacturers, retailers, or consumers on which color was feminine and which was masculine or whether they denoted gender at all' (Paoletti 2012: xviii). Yet, the use of color as a code for gender has become inscribed into our consciousness, to the point that we do not question whether this difference is due to nurture or nature – due to cultural upbringing, or genetics. In this way, gendered behavior is internalized and disciplined, enforced by the subjects of a given society. When viewed from this perspective, behaviors associated with a certain gender are seen as culturally, not biologically, determined. As Simone de Beauvoir puts it, 'One is not born, but rather becomes, a woman' (de Beauvoir 1973: 301).

Thus, Sarah's performance of the lyrics 'Take this pink ribbon from my eyes' is a lament about the expectations that Euro-American society holds over women, using karaoke to subvert traditional gender norms. This suggests that one of the keys to understanding the subversive potential of karaoke lies in using these performances to help unlock the arbitrary associations between material and performative culture. As Butler writes, 'The possibilities of gender transformation are to be found in the arbitrary relation between such acts, in the possibility of a different sort of repeating, in the breaking or subversive repetition of that style' (Butler 2007: 188).

Performing Relationships

Jessie and Lana are Wednesday night regulars. Jessie is the KJ at a nearby bar that has its karaoke nights on Tuesdays and Thursdays. Jessie is in his mid-forties, is of medium height, and is very skinny. He has a dark complexion, and short black hair with trimmed sideburns. Jessie typically dresses in all black, and tonight is no exception. He sports a black, long-sleeve dress shirt, black slacks, and black leather dress shoes. He also wears a small, circular, gold and maroon hat with a sewn-on patch of the Sanskrit character 'Om.' Lana is about the same age as Jessie. She wears a hat identical to Jessie's, and sports a long black-and-white dress covered with a floral pattern. Lana is a bit shorter and heavier than Jessie, wears glasses, and appears to be Caucasian. Jessie has picked the song 'One I Love,' by Wally Kurth, who in addition to playing in the band Kurth and Taylor is a star on the television soap opera *General Hospital*. Lana accompanies Jessie on stage, but she does not sing. As Jessie sings, his arm is draped around Lana's shoulders, and his gaze is directed squarely toward her. She returns his glances and smiles fondly, standing with her hands clasped together at her waistline. This song, which is also known as 'The General Hospital Song,' is a gentle country-style ballad. The lyrics are dripping with sentimentality, perhaps what one would expect from a song associated with a soap opera. The lyrics declare Jessie's undying love for Lana: 'Lay your soul down beside me/Let my touch soothe your fears/I'm not quite sure what tomorrow brings/But I'll always be here/You're the only one.' The sartorial choice of matching outfits, the choice of song, and the body language of the performers demonstrates how karaoke is sometimes used to perform a gendered relationship.

Drew observes that karaoke bars are 'fertile fields for courtship. [...] A guy who doesn't know a girl can walk up to her and say, "Hey, I'm really nervous about going up there, would you come up with me?" He can use it as an excuse to meet her. [...] As singing partners nominate tunes to perform, they can impress and appraise one another. [...] And as they perform, they can voice intensely personal sentiments under cover of song' (Drew 2001: 85). In addition to courtship, karaoke is a way for people to express all kinds of personal relationships, including those involving friendship, love, and family. Drew notes, 'Even when they sing in groups, celebrating and solidifying personal relationships, karaoke performers are driven to make those relationships public, to open them up to the world' (Drew 2001: 124). Thus, karaoke bars, in addition to being sites of commerce in terms of a place where physical goods are exchanged (primarily money for drinks and food), are also sites of commerce for romantic exchanges.

In my own ethnographic research of karaoke, I also found this to be true. I noticed that performances were often framed in terms of gendered relationships. That is, I observed sons and daughters expressing love for their fathers and mothers; fathers and mothers expressing their love for their daughters and sons; and husbands and boyfriends expressing love for their wives and girlfriends, and vice versa. In one of the interviews I conduct, Tom, the Saturday night KJ, tells me about how at one of his other gigs as a wedding KJ, he and his daughter sang together: 'Me and my daughter do this father/daughter thing at weddings. People love us. We're real cute.' I also observed countless performances of the dissolution of relationships, including performances of songs about break-ups and performances of songs about the loss of a loved one. In these cases, these relationships were nearly all framed in terms of gender differences.

Perhaps it is not surprising that many relationships have been spawned, nurtured, and even dissolved around the performance of karaoke. The connection between karaoke and romance is perhaps inevitable. Besides the fact that karaoke is typically performed in the same locations where hopeful romantics go to find and celebrate love, the content of karaoke songs is more likely to be about relationships than any other subject. This is because, in general, the content of popular music is this way. Donald Horton explores this subject in the 1990 article 'The Dialogue of Courtship in Popular Song.' Horton conducted an informal quantitative study of four music magazines from 1955: *Hit Parader*, *Song Hits Magazine*, *Country Song Roundup*, and *Rhythm and Blues*. These periodicals publish song lyrics from a variety of musical styles, including popular music, rock and roll, country, and R&B. The results showed that, almost unbelievably, 86.8% of the lyrics were, one way or another, related to the subject of love. Horton identifies what he calls '"scenes" in the drama of courtship' (Horton 1990: 15). These are, sequentially, 'Courtship,' 'The Honeymoon,' 'The Downward Curse of Love,' and, finally, 'All Alone.' He concludes that a reason the overwhelming majority of these song lyrics are about romance may be connected to the demographics of their typical audience (adolescent males), and the concern with issues related to the formation of identity during their formative years. He muses, 'The working-out of a socially valid and personally satisfactory conception of himself and his role in relation to the opposite sex is one of his most urgent and difficult tasks [...] the popular songs provide a language appropriate to such an identity' (Horton 1990: 26).

The function of romance in popular music is another issue that has been a hotly debated subject. Frith and McRobbie see romantic content in songs as a negative cultural force. In their discussion of 'teenybop' music (the binary flip-side of 'cock-rock,' marketed to and consumed mainly by females), they consider romantic content as a way to inculcate young females into the stereotypical roles that society imposes on them, in the domestic domain as wife and mother. They write, 'The dominant mode of control in popular music (the mode which is clearly embodied in teenybop culture) is the ideology of romance, which is itself the icing on the harsh ideology of domesticity' (Frith and McRobbie 1990: 387). Dyer, on the other hand, sees romance, a subject that is often explored in disco music, as a positive cultural force. For Dyer, the subject of romance, within the realm of leisure-time activities, provides a place where members of our society can explore alternatives to work and domesticity. He argues, 'For all its commercialism and containment within the to and fro between work and leisure, I think disco romanticism is one of the things that can keep the gap open, that can allow the *experience of contradiction* to continue' (Dyer 1990: 417, emphasis in original). It is precisely within these spaces of contradiction where the subversive nature of karaoke operates.

Subverting Gender

Consider that, quite often, the expression of relationships in popular music, and also in karaoke, is not restricted to heterosexual relationships. One evening at Capone's, I observe a karaoke performance in which a homosexual relationship is clearly being expressed, put on display, and declared to the world. There are many times when I notice various pairs of women sitting together, focused solely on each other, ignoring the advances of men. However, without being able to go up to the women and ask them, which would be very rude, I have no idea whether the women are friends or lovers. In one case, however, two women's relationship is made explicit through a series of performances.

On this occasion, one of two women sitting at a table near the stage, Lisa, gets up and sings the song 'Hotel California.' Lisa is an average looking woman in her early forties. She wears a red, long-sleeve flannel shirt and blue jeans. She has medium-length brown hair and wears glasses. As she sings, she directs her gaze toward the woman she was sitting with. The telling moment comes when she decides to change some of the lyrics of the song. The original version, as performed by The Eagles, goes, 'Her mind is Tiffany-twisted /She got the Mercedes bends/She got a lot of pretty, pretty boys, that she calls friends.' Instead, Lisa sings, while looking directly at the woman at the table, 'She got a lot of pretty, pretty girls, that she calls friends.' The woman at the table smiles back at Lisa. Suddenly, their relationship has become public, laid bare for the world to see. To be sure that I did not misinterpret this behavior, I continue to watch the two women as Lisa ends the song and goes back to the table. As she approaches the table, Lisa kisses the woman she was singing to on the lips, and sits down next to her with her arm around her. Lisa's performance has appropriated lyrics from a song that were originally a comment on a heteronormative relationship, and used them to destabilize the audience's preconceptions. This event demonstrates yet another way in which karaoke performances can subvert and destabilize traditional constructions of gendered relationships. Through a simple substitution of words inserted into the lyrics of a song by a karaoke performer, preconceptions toward gender and sexuality are stood on end.

The key to unraveling the debate over the position of gender in relation to popular music, oddly enough, may reside in the promise of karaoke as a subversive cultural force. I have already discussed examples of some of the ways that gender performance in karaoke can destabilize a fixed notion of gender. Further clues to the subversive possibilities of karaoke can be found in the passages of Reynolds and Press' book *The Sex Revolts* (1995), in their assessment of some of the strengths of the various approaches of women in rock music.

The first clue is found within a discussion of Madonna and what Lawrence Grossberg calls 'authentic inauthenticity.' While artists such as Bruce Springsteen and Tracy Chapman work hard to create a mirage of truth ('inauthentic authenticity'), Madonna is constantly reinventing herself, and celebrates the notions of a malleable identity. Reynolds and Press discuss the video of the song 'Vogue.' Madonna appropriated the concept of 'vogueing' from the subculture of drag balls held in New York City during the 1980s (documented in the Jennie Livingston film *Paris is Burning*). They explain, '"Vogue" preaches a secular gospel of self-reinvention and empowerment through mastery of surfaces: it's the punk idea of "anyone can do it," adapted for the Reagan-Bush era' (Reynolds and Press 1995: 319). In the video, after a series of shots that show Madonna in various poses portraying classic movie stars, she coyly sings, 'there's nothing to it.' Reynolds and Press argue, 'To take a Baudrillardian slant, maybe this "nothing" is what is subversive about vogueing: the idea that behind the shimmering surface of make-up and masquerade, there is no authentic identity. "Femininity" is deconstructed, revealed to be an array of attachments, additions and subtractions' (Reynolds and Press 1995: 321).

This assertion calls to mind Judith Butler's call-to-arms near the end of 'Performative Acts and Gender Constitution,' in which she imagines the possibility of future utopian responses to the problems she associates with the reification of gender norms: 'The prescription is invariably more difficult, if only because we need to think a world in which acts, gestures, the visual body, the clothed body, the various physical attributes usually associated with gender, *express nothing*' (Butler 2007: 197, emphasis in original). I offer that, similar to the concept of 'vogueing,' karaoke offers a similar space for such subversive possibilities to exist. Music critics often bemoan the lack of 'authenticity' in karaoke performance (the word 'karaoke' is perhaps the most-often used epithet to shame a poor singing performance on television shows such as *American Idol* and *The X-Factor*). Perhaps it is this lack of 'authenticity' that makes karaoke the perfect vehicle for a postmodern deconstruction of fixed notions of identity.

A second clue to the efficacy of karaoke as a subversive cultural force can be found in Reynolds and Press' discussion of the so-called 'Riot Grrrl' movement of the 1990s, exemplified by bands such as Bikini Kill, Huggy Bear, Bratmobile, and Sleater-Kinney. Similar to the punk rock music of the 1970s (but with an ear toward feminism rather than misogyny), the Riot Grrrl movement espoused the virtues of amateurism. Beat Happening was famous for their refusal to rehearse their performances, coming together only to play gigs and record their music. 'Riot Grrrls preach empowerment through forming bands and forming fanzines – it's the old punk DIY ethos of "anyone can do it," but with a feminist twist (they're rejecting masculine notions of expertise and mastery)' (Reynolds and Press 1995: 324). Critics of the Riot Grrrl movement (including Reynolds and Press) complain that this lack of virtuosity ultimately led the Riot Grrrl movement to become a footnote on the tome of rock history. But they also admit:

> But a rock critical perspective – one that evaluates the music in terms of innovation, formal excellence, etc. – is highly inappropriate when it comes to Riot Grrrl. These women are not necessarily *interested* in making a contribution to rock history or the evolution of the form. Riot Grrrl is foremost about process, not product; it's about the empowerment that comes from 'getting up and doing it,' and the inspiration audience members draw from witnessing this spectacle of self-liberation.
>
> (Reynolds and Press 1995: 327–328, emphasis in original)

Karaoke performance shares the same 'anyone can do it' ethos as punk and Riot Grrrl. Performers of karaoke are not concerned with changing the face of history. Karaoke performances are about process, not product.

Thus, I suggest that karaoke may be the perfect solution to the challenge of creating a new, feminist form of creating music that pushes the boundaries of form, and not just content. Perhaps, in the emulation of karaoke as a subversive form of performance, other cultural forms might be invented to provide a similar approach toward the same end. Rather than trying to reinvent aspects of musical production that are properties inherently bound to the process of its production, we must continue to appropriate the ways in which music, as well as other forms of art, entertainment, and an unlimited variety of cultural products, is consumed. Picking up a microphone and stepping out on stage is the first step of an active consumer who can break away from the confinement of the system, and use the products of the structure in a new, resistant way.

Figure 1: The Shinjuku district in Tokyo, Japan.

Figure 2: The exterior of a karaoke establishment in Tokyo, Japan.

Figure 3: The author sings karaoke with a live band in Tokyo, Japan.

Figure 4: A video screen in a karaoke establishment in Shanghai, China.

Figure 5: Friends sing in a karaoke box in Shanghai, China.

Figure 6: 'Crashing' a karaoke box in Shanghai, China.

Figure 7: The aftermath of a karaoke party.

Figure 8: Friends sing karaoke at a bar in Missouri, United States.

Chapter 4

Paint It Black

I see a red door and I want it painted black.
No colors any more, I want them to turn black.

– The Rolling Stones

Not many people know his real name, but his karaoke name is 'Guns.' The regulars at Capone's gave him this moniker because of his long, muscular arms. On each of them, he sports a different tattoo. On his left arm is a green outline of a four-leaf clover, about four inches long in each direction. On the right arm is a green tracing of a tall beer mug with the word 'Guinness' inscribed on it. When I ask him what the tattoos are about, he explains to me, 'I'm Irish.' Guns is the next singer. Today he is wearing a white tank top that shows off his huge biceps and tattoos. He has decided to sing the song 'Whiskey in the Jar,' a traditional Irish folk song. The karaoke version of the song, however, is performed in the style of a cover by the heavy metal rock band 'Metallica.' Guns grabs the microphone and holds it strongly in his left hand. Because he is a regular karaoke singer, he has a good, practiced voice.

His tone is smooth, but every once in a while he lapses into the harsh, crackling overtones of the voice of Metallica singer James Hetfield. The song is about an Irish highwayman who robs an English military officer. It begins, 'As I was goin' over the Cork and Kerry Mountains/I saw Captain Farrell and his money he was counting/I first produced my pistol and then produced my rapier/I said, "Stand and deliver or the devil he may take ya."' This song originated in the seventeenth century, and has become one of the most popular Irish folk songs of all time. The connection to Ireland is invoked in the song by the mentioning of names and features of the Irish landscape. It is common for folk songs to mention geographical locations as markers of identity, but the deeper 'Irish' meaning of the song resonates with the revolutionary attitude that marks the spirit of the Irish as a people subjugated to colonialism.

It seems perfect that the song should be sung again here at Capone's, the namesake and atmosphere of which invoke a revolutionary, anti-authoritarian spirit. To paraphrase a local restaurant critic, 'Capone's is a place with a "bad ass" attitude.' The performance of this song by Guns echoes this spirit, with his 'Irish' tattoos and his tight fitting shirt that seems ready-made for showing off features of his masculinity. His choice of song and the messages inscribed on his arm mark him as something else as well, as 'Irish.' But Guns is not actually Irish – not exactly. He explains, 'My grandfather came to America from Ireland before I was born, so I've got Irish 'blood' in me. My mother's side of the family was from Germany. My father told me stories about growing up in Ireland.' When I ask Guns whether he has ever been to Ireland, he flatly admits, 'no.'

Deconstructing Race

Stories like that of Guns' are common in today's society, especially in the United States, where generations of immigration have resulted in a shuffling of a multiethnic landscape, the stuff of which the postmodern condition is made. Performances of ethnicity, which once seemed 'authentic' in some parts of the world where the forces of globalization had not fully taken hold, are increasingly more difficult to ascertain as 'authentic' in any discernible way. The continuing worldwide merging of economic, political, and cultural values is repainting the cultural landscape. Nowhere is this clearer than in the United States, where performances of ethnicity like the one just described are the norm, not the exception. Although Guns has attempted to mark his Irish ethnicity through getting Irish tattoos and singing Irish folk songs, there is not really any way one can claim that Guns' performance is authentically 'Irish.' Still, if you asked Guns, he would tell you that his ethnicity is very real to him.

First, consider another question, is there really such a thing as 'race'? Race has become a difficult topic to discuss in today's over-politicized world. Although the United States has, for the first time in history, elected a President with African American heritage, racial tensions in the United States and other parts of the world seem to be escalating at an alarming pace. This is why it has become so urgent to have a frank discussion about this issue. Perhaps by coming to a better understanding of the way that cultural differences are constructed, we can begin to put these perceived differences behind us.

You will notice in this chapter that I have chosen to use the term 'ethnicity' instead of 'race.' I prefer to use the term 'ethnicity' because the word 'race' implies a genetic, essentialist connection between biological factors and behavior. The word 'ethnicity,' on the other hand, denotes cultural factors rather than biological factors when considering the formation of certain human behaviors. It is only through the performance of behaviors that are associated with certain ethnic groups that the concept of race becomes 'naturalized,' that is, assumed to be a result of biological, genetic factors. The question is, then, whether ethnicity is entirely a cultural phenomenon. My goal in this chapter is not to 'solve' the problems associated with discussions of race and ethnicity. In fact, my goal is to further problematize this discourse in order to convince the reader that perceived racial differences are the result of an overactive cultural imagination.

In Search of a Voice

One of the most important ethnographic studies of karaoke is Casey Man Kong Lum's *In Search of a Voice: Karaoke and the Construction of Identity in Chinese America* (1996). Lum's ethnography is a very useful resource when considering topics that are at the intersection of karaoke and the formation of ethnicity. Lum writes about the performance of karaoke in three distinct ethnic communities around the New York and New Jersey area. In the case of Lum's case studies, we see how ethnic communities come together through the power of karaoke. We also begin to notice that various cultural groups each have a different way of performing karaoke. Perhaps this is due to the way that a Geertzian 'deep structure' of culture permeates these performances.

Although all three of the communities that Lum studies are Asian American, there are further divisions within each community in terms of economic class, and sometimes subtle regional differences as well. One is a community of immigrants from Hong Kong that use karaoke to share their love of Cantonese Opera, one is a community where Taiwanese immigrants use karaoke as a way to display their wealth, and one is a community where Malaysian immigrants use karaoke as a means of escape. Lum borrows literary critic Stanly Fish's (1980) term 'interpretive communities' to describe these three enclaves where he observed performances of karaoke. Lum writes, 'The karaoke practices of the three interpretive communities, including their specific choices of music, are expressions of the distinct ethnic and regional backgrounds of the people as they construct and maintain social membership' (Lum 1996: 101–102).

Lum paraphrases Fish's definition of interpretive community as 'The sum of people who experience a text according to a frame of reference commonly shared among them' (Lum 1996: 20). Lum explains his reason for adopting Fish's paradigm: 'First, the field research on which this book is based indicates that people who congregate in similar dramaturgical sites tend to share social, economic, and ethnic backgrounds. Second, people who congregate in their preferred karaoke scenes tend to use karaoke to similar ends. Third, [...] people congregating in karaoke scenes play an active role in the construction and appropriation of meanings' (Lum 1996: 20).

In the case of the immigrants from Hong Kong, Lum hypothesizes, 'The cultural practice of singing Cantonese opera songs in karaoke in this community reflects a negotiation between two media and cultural forms – two articulations of life, whereby a certain form of regional folklore, artistry, and ritual from a bygone era is being reframed and reclaimed in a contemporary, diasporic, and technological environment' (Lum 1996: 53). In the case of the Taiwanese community, Lum concludes, 'karaoke-related objects and activities are used in this interpretive community as a means to display and express people's wealth and social class' (Lum 1996: 69). In the case of the Malaysian migrant workers, Lum explains, 'The use of karaoke here speaks to people's need to have an escape, or therapeutic mechanism, that gives them access to a way of life otherwise absent from their everyday existence' (Lum 1996: 97). In the end of Lum's study, he notes that, even though each of these ethnic communities uses karaoke in a different way, the people who form these communities share a common experience as Asian Americans. He concludes, 'The frame of reference they bring with them – their past experiences, their aspirations – allows them not only to adopt to the new environments, but also redefine and shape them. In the process, they build communities, they construct identities in relation to others, and they establish a voice of their own' (Lum 1996: 113). Lum continually reiterates the central theme of his book, the idea that karaoke performance provides people with a way to have a 'voice' in their community.

The Big Easy

Although most of my time studying karaoke is spent at Capone's, occasionally I am presented with opportunities to see the karaoke establishments of other cities in the United States and abroad. One of these experiences happens while I am in New Orleans for an academic conference during the late summer of 2007. It is two years after Hurricane Katrina devastated the city. I will never forget riding on the shuttle from the airport to my hotel, seeing entire neighborhoods shrouded in complete darkness, without electricity. Like many big cities in the southern United States, which still feel the reverberation of the history of slavery and segregation, there remain invisible lines dividing different parts of the city. Unfortunately, the destruction caused by the storm was not felt equally among the various ethnic groups that call the city their home. Neighborhoods where the majority of the people are white, usually the more affluent, seemed to be spared from the worst of Katrina. After the storm, the break in the levees allowed the storm surge to flow into neighborhoods built at lower elevations, which happen to be where many minorities live. The part of the town where I am staying, the French Quarter, experienced some hardship, but was quickly rebuilt, perhaps because a lot of money is brought in along Bourbon Street by the tourists who frequent the many bars and nightclubs there. What happens next is an experience that provides an example of stark contrasts in the way that ethnicity is sometimes performed within different subcultures.

The French Quarter is an area of town that, in contrast to many of the other ethnic neighborhoods of the city, boasts a large amount of diversity in the ethnicities of the people who spend time there. I have flown in the night before the conference. After I settle into my hotel, I walk to Bourbon Street to take in some of the nightlife, and see if I can find a karaoke bar. The first bar that I walk into is a 'cowboy' themed bar. In the center of the bar is a large 'corral,' built with slats of wooden fencing. In the middle of the corral is a large, mechanical bull. People are not riding the bull tonight, because it is karaoke night. All along the walls of the bar, there are various bits of scenery and props that connect to the 'western' theme. The room is brightly lit with warm colors, mostly reds, yellows, and oranges. The walls of the bar are made of faux-wood paneling. There are countless skulls of dead animals hung on the wall, observing the patrons with their eerie grins. There are rings of rolled-up, rusted barbed wire. There are various pieces of cowboy clothing and paraphernalia, including cowboy boots, spurs, cowboy hats, chaps, and Sheriff's stars, all hung in different parts of the bar as decoration. Beyond the visual elements, the aural dimension also plays into the 'cowboy' theme, consisting mostly of country music. Oddly enough, the patrons of this bar are not dressed in a way that reflects the theme. They are predominately young people – most appear to be in their twenties and thirties. They are dressed in outfits ranging from casual to semi-formal, but in very typical attire for going out in the city, with men in dress shirts and chinos, and women in blouses and short skirts or sun dresses. Although there is some diversity in the crowd, the clientele is predominantly white.

It is very common for karaoke night to start with a performance by the KJ. In a similar way to 'opening bands' at rock concerts, this serves to loosen up the audience and get things rolling early in the night when not all of the regular singers have arrived yet. The KJ is a young man in his mid-thirties. Unlike the people in the crowd, his clothes match the 'cowboy' theme of the bar. He wears blue jeans held up by a belt with a conspicuously large buckle, a red-and-white, checkered, long-sleeved shirt (despite the heat), a brown leather vest, and a black cowboy hat. He has chosen to open the karaoke set with the song 'Save a Horse (Ride a Cowboy),' by the band Big & Rich. He sings, 'Well, I walk into the room, passing out hundred dollar bills, and it kills and it thrills like the horns on my Silverado grill/ And I buy the bar a double round of crown, and everybody's getting down, an' this town ain't never gonna be the same.' The song features a danceable beat, in a genre somewhere between club music and country. Soon the dance floor is packed with gyrating bodies.

After I leave the cowboy bar, I walk further down Bourbon Street. Less than a block away from the first location, I wander into what could be described as a 'hip hop' themed club. The ambiance of the bar is quite subdued compared to the cowboy bar. The room is dimly lit, with subtle shades of blue and purple. There are red-and-green neon lights shining along the side of the bar. The decor on the walls consists of abstract, modern paintings, featuring splashes of color in nondescript patterns. The furniture in the bar is very nice and upscale: stools with faux leopard-skin covers at the bar and leather-bound lounge chairs along the walls, and comfy booths in the corners. Loud music with a heavy bass beat is playing in the background.

The clientele of the bar is ethnically diverse, although the majority of the people here are African American. I make my way to the back of the bar and find a hallway to a back room with a large dance floor. Some of the patrons lounge and talk quietly in the booths. Others dance, some in groups, some as couples, and some alone. There are disco-style, flashing lights illuminating the dance floor, providing a somewhat chaotic scene. The last song ends and an emcee comes out from behind a curtain at the edge of the stage. He announces into the microphone, 'It's time for the Cupid Shuffle. Y'all get out here!' The 'Cupid Shuffle' is a song by R&B artist Cupid (a.k.a. Bryson Bernard). As the song begins, the emcee sings along over the prerecorded soundtrack, periodically giving instructions to the dancing crowd. It is not karaoke, exactly, but perhaps qualifies as karaoke's close cousin.

There is a sudden stirring at the edge of the bar, as some of the patrons who were sitting quietly erupt with excitement and make their way to the floor. The emcee sings the lyrics along with Cupid's recorded voice, 'They say I'm a rapper, and I say no/They say what you doing tryna do some zydeco (hey)/I just let the music come from my soul/So all of my people can stay on the floor (ooh ooh)/They got a brand new dance (come on), you gotta move your muscle/Brand new dance, it's called the Cupid Shuffle.' As the song nears the chorus, the people on the dance floor form into a line. What I begin to experience, for the first time in my sheltered life, is a hip hop line dance. The lyrics of the chorus consist of instructions for the dance, and every line has its own move. It goes, 'To the right, to the right, to the right, to the right/To the left, to the left, to the left, to the left/Now kick, now kick, now kick, now kick/Now walk it by yourself, now walk it by yourself.' I always thought of line dancing as something more likely to occur in a country bar, more like the 'cowboy' bar that I experienced previously. But here in this club, I see the same kind of phenomenon. It is a line dance, but culturally transposed to a hip hop sensibility.

What strikes me most about this experience is how these bars represent vastly contrasting performances of ethnicity. How exactly this phenomenon comes about is a haunting question. Somehow, like the larger city of New Orleans, and despite the fact that people of many different ethnicities are found in the French Quarter, the bars I visit seem to be segregated largely by ethnic affiliation. I am not talking about an enforced segregation, as was the case in many parts of the South before the civil rights movement of the 1960s, but some kind of self-segregation, enforced by cultural forces that have been internalized and disciplined by the people themselves. The division is not total, as I observe people of all ethnicities in these locations, but the phenomenon is noticeable. I am not sure why this happens, other than to speculate that they are the remains of invisible cultural fault lines, haunted by the ghosts of history. Beyond this possibility, it is very probable that people of different ethnicities are drawn to locations where there are people like them.

In this example, I have provided a thick description of two different sites of cultural performance. In this case, I have compared and contrasted a 'cowboy bar' and a 'hip hop club.' When one analyzes these performances from a dramaturgical perspective, one can appreciate the unique differences in cultural aesthetics, in terms of 'setting,' 'costume,' 'lighting,' and 'sound.' The 'actors' and 'audience' also have distinctive qualities. It just so happens that these two bars are popular with members of two distinct subcultures that can be differentiated by, although not exclusively, ethnicity. Beyond this particular example, I could just have easily analyzed a variety of cultural sites, localities for many kinds of subcultures, demarcated by performances of identity related to gender, class, age, religion, or a number of other factors. The common denominator is a kind of in-group/out-group behavior that I observed in a number of different locations during my study. The separation is not enforced in any kind of official way. This making of community is determined, disciplined, and inscribed through unspoken rules, in this case, marked by performances of ethnicity.

All Over the World

One book that explores connections between karaoke and ethnicity in many different countries is *Karaoke: The Global Phenomenon* (2007) by Zhou Xun and Francesca Tarocco. This book provides a virtual tour of karaoke performance around the world. It uses the performance of karaoke as a way to talk about many diverse cultures. What is perhaps most striking is the realization of how pervasive the performance of karaoke has become in various countries all over the world. Karaoke, as the title of the book suggests, has truly become a global phenomenon. Although karaoke started out in Japan and quickly spread around various countries in Asia, it took many years for karaoke to spread around the world. Today, after several decades, it is now performed in virtually every corner of the globe, from São Paulo to Melbourne, from Kashgar to Istanbul. Exploring the way that karaoke is performed in these various countries provides insight into the ways different types of cultural meanings become associated with karaoke in different countries. In this way, a study of karaoke around the world becomes a study of ethnicity around the world.

Xun and Tarocco explain the scope of their project, 'In each of these places karaoke adopts different features and characteristics, and takes on cultural-specific meanings and symbolisms' (Xun and Tarocco 2007: 28). Each chapter visits different countries around the world. For example, in Korea the chief editor of *The Korean Times*, Moo-jong Park, 'once declared singing the "national sport" of Korea. [...] Almost every Korean, he claimed, has a fair-to-good-to-excellent singing voice' (Park qtd. in Xun and Tarocco 2007: 47). Obviously, this is an overstatement, but Koreans seem to be very serious about karaoke. According to Xun and Tarocco, 'Many Koreans claim that the karaoke box originated in Korea, not Japan' (Xun and Tarocco 2007: 48).

Strangely, ethnic conflicts over karaoke innovations have erupted in other parts of the world as well. Once a man in the Philippines, Roberto del Rosario, complained of patent infringement by a Chinese company, saying that he had invented a karaoke machine in 1975. 'On 15 March 1996 the Supreme Court in the Philippines ruled in favor of Del Rosario, making him the world's sole patent holder for the karaoke system' (Xun and Tarocco 2007: 19). Even though Rosario won his patent case in the Philippines, most scholars recognize that karaoke was invented by Daisuke Inoue, a Japanese man, in 1971. In the Philippines, 'karaoke is so fundamental to their life that owning a karaoke machine is far more important than having a toilet in their home' (Xun and Tarocco 2007: 77). One of the most popular artists there is Frank Sinatra, and all of the karaoke machines are packed with music made famous by Sinatra. 'The Filipinos are proud, dramatic, defiant, emotional, yet tolerant and forgiving, and "My Way" is their perfect song: "I've had my fill, my share of losing... And now... as tears subside... I find it all, so amusing"' (Xun and Tarocco 2007: 79).

In fact, the song 'My Way,' originally written by Paul Anka for Sinatra, is at the center of a Philippine urban legend called 'The My Way Killings.' Supposedly, around the turn of the millennium, singing the song in karaoke bars in the Philippines led to a string of murders. The song now has a strange taboo attached to it, and has been banned from many bars that have gone so far as to remove the song entirely from their playlists. No one knows exactly how many people have died because of the song, but the newspapers have reported at least half a dozen or more killings. It is not clear why violence seems to follow the song. Some people have hypothesized that it is because of the popularity of the song. Because it is sung so often, it is only coincidentally related to incidents of violence. Others have blamed the theme of the song, which can be interpreted as condoning excessive pride. Butch Albarracin, owner of a Manila singing school, tries to explain, '"I did it my way" — it's so arrogant [...] The lyrics evoke feelings of pride and arrogance in the singer, as if you're somebody when you're really nobody. It covers up your failures. That's why it leads to fights' (Albarracin qtd. in Onishi 2010: A6). Other theories blame the difficulty of the song. Because everyone has an opinion on how the song should be sung, bad singers are more likely to be criticized and violence ensues. Whether or not this urban legend is actually true, this strange anecdote demonstrates how specific meanings can be connected to karaoke performances within a particular culture.

In Thailand, karaoke has been used to unite the people of Issan, a minority group that lives in Thailand on the border with Laos. The Issan hold the annual Phi Ta Khon festival. The festival features dancing (*Khon* dances originated from *Nang* shadow theater performances) and karaoke; it is 'a real sing-along fiesta' (Xun and Tarocco 2007: 66). A sense of unity is felt among the Issan people as they sing their epic Morlan songs. Xun and Tarocco explain, 'The lyrics are sung in the Issan dialect and those in the audience who originally came from Issan to work in the modern metropolis respond in the same. As the music takes hold, they often increasingly begin to feel "back home"' (Xun and Tarocco 2007: 67). This revival of cultural traditions is only possible because karaoke is a technology of music and song, which are social forces that have the power to bring people together. Time and again, the karaoke literature is filled with examples of diaspora and return, where karaoke becomes a means by which a group of people connect together despite their separation from a homeland.

In Brazil, for example, there are about 1.2 million Japanese immigrants. Their descendants are called Nikkeijin, which literally means 'sun line people' (Xun and Tarocco 2007: 159). The Nikkeijin have a dual identity: in Brazil they are considered Japanese, and they are looked upon as a minority. In Japan, Nikkeijin who either travel to or have moved back to Japan are considered 'foreigners' (*gaijin*). This dual identity is played out in their performances of karaoke: in Nikkeijin communities in Brazil, Japanese-style karaoke is more popular, while the karaoke performed in Nikkeijin communities in Japan has more of a Brazilian influence. Xun and Tarocco tell us, 'As for karaoke, if the members of the Brazilian Nikkei community love to sing Japanese songs, in Japan, by contrast, they give heartfelt renditions of Brazilian songs' (Xun and Tarocco 2007: 163). In a way this makes perfect sense, especially if one understands the performance of karaoke as a way for people to connect to their ethnic identity. In both cases, the diaspora creates a need to feel connected to the place from where they have traveled, the place to which they still feel a connection. The music becomes a proxy for home.

While karaoke has the power to unite people who have been separated over long distances, the power of karaoke has also been harnessed for other, less benign purposes. For example, karaoke has also been used for political purposes in China. A controversial report in a 1994 issue of *Asia.INC* reported that the majority of karaoke bars in Shanghai 'were owned, wholly or partly, by the Public Security Bureau (China's national police force) and by the People's Liberation Army' (Xun and Tarocco 2007: 99). If this is true, and considering that karaoke is a multibillion dollar industry in China, then the Public Security Bureau (PSB) and People's Liberation Army (PLA) are being partially funded by money generated from the performance of karaoke.

Karaoke bars have also become a controversial subject in Tibet, where the Chinese government has been accused of setting up karaoke bars as a way to spread Chinese culture and do away with Tibetan culture. Xun and Tarocco explain, 'Many observers claim that

China is swamping Tibetan culture in a number of ways, including ruthless modernization' (Xun and Tarocco 2007: 177). Activists who support Tibetan independence have accused China of an 'undercover war' against Tibetan Buddhism. 'Tibet, the mystical Buddhist land, the "land of snow," that bastion of the western Orientalist vision of otherness and the frontier, is now truly a "karaoke land"' (Xun and Tarocco 2007: 179).

In Vietnam, the power of karaoke is also used for political ends. The Co people of the Tra Bong district in Quang Ngai have used songs by Vietnamese composer Trinh Cong Son to stir up patriotism and to inspire ethnic uprisings. These songs are still available because of karaoke, and singing them can awaken feelings of nationalism. Xun and Tarocco write:

> As a patriotic tool, karaoke has the power to unite. It also has the ability to enhance social harmony and preserve lost traditions. In Vietnam, as in other parts of Asia, karaoke often becomes the place where the old meets the young, tradition meets modernity: when all the generations of the family sit together in front of the karaoke machine to sing and share their love and nostalgia, lost music is often revived through this modern media.
>
> (Xun and Tarocco 2007: 83–84)

Whether the power of karaoke is being used to unite people, or whether it is being used for political purposes, it is undeniable that karaoke allows people to create and reinforce ethnic boundaries. As a technology of music, karaoke is a technology of identity formation. Karaoke enables the performance of songs that are meaningful to people in terms of their membership in specific social groups. 'Karaoke enhances social bonding: community is the key. At these venues there is often a sense of group solidarity, a "membership," that gives all participants a feeling of shared identity, security and mutual support' (Xun and Tarocco 2007: 125). In this way, performances of karaoke enable the formation of communities.

Keeping It Real

Timmy is an African American male in his middle twenties. He is wearing a light, powder-blue sweater with thin white horizontal stripes and navy-blue, nylon sweat pants with a white vertical stripe on the outside seams. He wears white leather tennis shoes; has short, dark, curly hair; and there is a small gold stud earring in his left ear. Timmy has chosen to sing 'Sexual Healing,' by Marvin Gaye. As the first few notes of the song sound out, he grabs hold of the microphone with his left hand and gently holds it sideways at the corner of his mouth. He sings, 'Get up, get up, get up, get up/Wake up, wake up, wake up , wake up/Oh baby, now let's get down tonight.' Timmy's voice is not very strong and he struggles to raise his voice to the high pitch of the original singer.

As he gets further into the song, Timmy begins to feel the music, and sways his hips from left to right. He bobs his head to the side in rhythm to the beat, his ear gently brushing his shoulder and gently snapping back. He makes eye contact with one of the girls sitting at my table, a young woman in her early thirties. He sings directly to her as he motions with his hand toward his crotch: 'Come take control/Just grab a hold/Of my body and mind/Soon we'll be making it.' Timmy moves his karaoke performance to a table of two women across the dance floor from us, and begins courting both of them at the same time. His demeanor is playful and flirtatious, but he is also quite sincere in his rendition of the song. Although his performance is amateurish, it is touching. What Timmy lacks in natural singing talent he makes up for with his determination.

I include the example of Timmy because it points to one of the problems I encountered with my analysis of ethnicity in karaoke. Although it is clear that Timmy is African American, there is not a single particular part of Timmy's performance that directly refers to his ethnicity. It would be a mistake to attribute the nuances of his performance to the color of his skin. That would be recapitulating essentialism, just another attempt to 'naturalize' cultural distinctions by attributing them to biological origins. This is the subtle difference between 'race' and 'ethnicity.' 'Race' is assumed to be of genetic origin, although that notion has been disproved scientifically. Ethnicity, on the other hand, has very little to do with race itself, if anything at all. There is nothing in Timmy's performance that can be labeled as an 'authentic' performance of ethnicity. Perhaps, at least, one could describe Timmy's performance as 'sincere.'

'Racial sincerity,' as differentiated from 'racial authenticity,' is discussed at length in John L. Jackson's ethnography *Real Black: Adventures in Racial Sincerity*. Jackson writes, 'Sincerity and authenticity have very different ways of imagining the real, different ways of "keeping it real," and so *racial* sincerity, which should not be confused with *racial* authenticity, exemplifies an epistemologically distinct rendering of race, identity, solidarity, and reality' (Jackson 2005: 12, emphasis in original). Jackson concedes that the difference between sincerity and authenticity, at least for some, may seem like mere semantics. Jackson acknowledges and explores the problems inherent in differentiating sincerity from authenticity. Nevertheless, parsing the terms is a step in the right direction in terms of overcoming essentialism and the 'objectification' of the racial subject. He writes, 'A mere object could never be sincere, even if it is authentic. [...] Questions of sincerity imply social interlocutors who presume one another's humanity, interiority, and subjectivity' (Jackson 2005: 15). Thus, at least within a discursive context, perhaps it is preferable to discuss 'performances of sincerity' rather than 'performances of authenticity.'

White Rock/Black Roll

Normative performances of ethnicity, such as normative performances of gender, can be subverted. As previously discussed, in his *Glam Rock* book, Philip Auslander uses a paradigm of gender performance based on the theories of Judith Butler to deconstruct 'feminine' performances of male rock stars. The example of David Bowie permits us to transfer arguments that Auslander makes about the subject of gender to the subject of ethnicity.

Bowie is oftentimes credited as the 'father' of glam rock. Auslander explains that, because Bowie had a background in stage acting before he became a rock icon, his performance style was rooted in theatricality. Auslander explains, 'I suggest that his basic assumptions concerning rock performance were analogous to those of a stage actor in that he saw himself moving from role to role rather than developing a single persona' (Auslander 2006: 107). Born David Jones, his first theatrical act as a rock artist was to adopt 'David Bowie' as his stage name. In addition to this nominal layer of identity, Bowie began to accumulate more alter egos, first becoming 'Ziggy Stardust,' a guitar-playing alien from Mars. With his blatant bisexuality, Ziggy was a perfect emblem for glam rock because of his subversion of gender norms. As any stage actor eventually grows tired of a role, Bowie moved on from Ziggy Stardust and adopted a new role, that of 'The Thin White Duke.' With this new identity, Bowie would shift his performative protest of normative sexuality to a performative protest of normative ethnicity.

The backstory of The Thin White Duke is that he is a young, white, British boy who lives out a fantasy of being black. In his move from the character of Ziggy to the character of The Thin White Duke, many theatrical aspects of Bowie's performances began to shift as well. Auslander describes a performance of the song 'Young Americans' by Bowie on *The Dick Cavett Show* in 1974:

> He wore a light brown suit with exaggeratedly padded shoulders and high-waisted trousers from which a long chain looped down, zoot suit style, on his right side; white shoes; a blue shirt; and a tie. [...] If Ziggy's voice was a high, somewhat nasal, head voice, this singer's voice was deeper, huskier, throatier. Whereas Ziggy's posture was erect yet relaxed, this singer seemed to carry tension in his shoulders, his head jutting from his shoulders like a vulture's. [...] The music was not rock music, exactly, but a version of African-American soul and disco. None of the Spiders from Mars was there; the singer was accompanied largely by African-American musicians and a sextet of backup singers.
>
> (Auslander 2006: 148)

Because Auslander's book is about the performance of gender, his exploration of Bowie's new ethnic persona ends with the debut of The Thin White Duke, but some other information that Auslander tells us about the history of rock music provides a backdrop for what Bowie may have been up to with this new character.

Glam rockers such as Bowie, Marc Bolan, and Suzi Quatro attempted to call attention to a double standard of sexism in the world of psychedelic rock, and by extension illuminate some of the contradictions in the countercultural movement of the late 1960s and early 1970s. Although the counterculture supposedly embraced liberal ideals of equality, their approach to sexuality was quite germane. It is true that there was a degree to which ideals of masculinity and femininity were softened through an embracing of androgynous images, but there was also sometimes an undercurrent of homophobia in rock and countercultural ideology. In a directly parallel way, the treatment of gender by the counterculture was similar to their treatment of ethnicity. In a footnote, Auslander discusses the 'color line' in the history of popular music, which is related to the differences in the genres of 'rock' versus 'rock 'n' roll':

> The 'whiteness' of rock is one of the things that distinguish it from its precursor, rock and roll, a majority of whose performers were African-American. White rock and rollers like Jerry Lee Lewis and Elvis Presley were often said to have imitated black vocal and performance styles. The fact that a few very successful and popular psychedelic rock musicians, such as Carlos Santana, Sly Stone, and Jimi Hendrix, were not white should not be allowed to obscure the more salient fact that people of color were actively discouraged from seeking high visibility as rock musicians.
>
> (Auslander 2006: 31)

When viewed in the light of historical information pertaining to the general exclusion of black artists in psychedelic rock, Bowie's invention of The Thin White Duke can be understood as his attempt to take glam rock's protests against rock's ideology of normative sexuality into the realm of ethnicity.

The case of The Thin White Duke highlights a problem that has to do with the production of culture and the concept of 'authenticity.' In fact, it demonstrates how the very notion of 'authenticity' is a highly problematic concept in and of itself. As evidence of the way that the color line has been enforced between musical genres, consider the case of the African American act The Chambers Brothers and their hit 'Time Has Come Today,' discussed by Auslander in *Liveness: Performance in a Mediatized Culture*: 'The record companies interested in signing them wanted to treat them as an "R&B act with uniforms and choreography." Columbia Records, with whom the Chambers Brothers did sign, did not place that demand on them but said that "Time Has Come Today" could only be recorded by a White rock group' (Auslander 1999: 67). Eventually, Columbia did let the Chambers Brothers record their song, but only after they had a hit record. Auslander continues, 'In the 1970s, the Chambers were remanded by Columbia to the R&B producers Gamble and Huff, who attempted to make them over into a "Black" act' (Auslander 1999: 67). The story of the Chambers Brothers is but one told story from perhaps thousands of untold stories in the history of cultural production. The stark fact is that record company executives, promoters, and agents practice cultural production in the music industry. This was true during the early formation of rock 'n' roll in the 1950s, continued into the 1960s and 1970s, and is still practiced today.

The ethnic schism between the genres of rock 'n' roll and rock would turn out to be a watershed moment in race politics in the music industry. From that point on, musical acts would often be (but not always) signed, promoted, and retained by labels on the basis of whether they were considered a 'black act' or a 'white act.' This practice of cultural production highlights the importance of the concept of 'genres' in the music industry. In

Rockin' Out: Popular Music in the USA, Reebee Garofalo writes, 'The marketing categories of the music industry have often classified performers as much by race as by musical style' (Garofalo 1997: 9). Genre divisions, and the ethnic divisions that follow, have continued until the present day. Record stores are divided into sections such as 'rock,' 'pop,' 'country,' 'urban,' and 'salsa.' Although the implication of this division is not immediately apparent, the subliminal message is undeniable. At least in the minds of a majority of marketers and producers, the 'genres' (or kinds) of music parallel genres (or kinds) of identity. Garofalo explains, 'The beginnings of this practice date back to the 1920s, when the music industry organized popular music into three categories: "race" (African American popular music), "hillbilly" (white, working-class rural styles), and "popular" (mainstream pop of the type produced by Tin Pan Alley)' (Garofalo 1997: 9). Even today, marketing executives seem to tailor products to given demographics: 'rock' is primarily marketed toward white males; 'pop' music is primarily marketed toward females; 'urban' music is marketed to African Americans; and 'salsa' is marketed to Latinos.

The question is, to what degree does the division of music into different genres take place on an organic, 'authentic' basis? Furthermore, have the associations between specific genres and specific ethnicities arisen in a natural way? In other words, do images in the media reflect organic culture or does organic culture reflect images in the media? Once again, we find a connection between ethnicity and 'authenticity' that is problematic. This is a 'chicken and egg' problem, and there is no easy answer to this paradoxical issue. Complicating the issue is the fact that the majority of the people who make decisions about which genre a band belongs in are white. In the book *Music Genres and Corporate Cultures*, Keith Negus writes, 'Although numerous African-American executives have contributed to the formation of the modern music industry and the history of recorded popular music, all have continued to occupy a "precarious position"' (Sanjek qtd. in Negus 1999: 89). The precarious position of these executives stems from the trend that, although there are often African American executives in charge of the so-called 'black' division of many record companies, they are usually in middle-management positions and not in charge of decisions such as restructuring, shuffling personnel, or occasionally shutting down these divisions altogether. Garofalo laments, 'Black personnel have been systematically excluded from positions of power within the industry' (Garofalo 1994: 275).

The same problems that complicate the landscape of cultural production in the music industry are found in karaoke as well. Karaoke songs are often released by the same record company that originally produced the music, or the songs are licensed by karaoke production companies that may hire a studio band to reproduce the music without lyrics for the sole purpose of distribution via various karaoke media, including laser discs, CD+Gs, and MP3+Gs, over proprietary computer networks and the Internet. In Japan, the release of a new song is often coordinated with the release of its karaoke version, either within days, hours, or sometimes simultaneously with the release of the original song. Now, karaoke is even available via iTunes and Facebook. Using these new media technologies keeps the production of karaoke linked in to the most cutting-edge methods of distribution and reproduction in the music industry. As a technology of the new media, karaoke has become another method of cultural production. In the case of karaoke, as in the case of popular music, ethnicity is 'produced.'

Us and Them

A group comprising two men and two women in their mid-thirties approaches the stage. They are all dressed in matching white-and-blue softball uniforms, complete with baseball caps and black leather cleats. It seems that they have come to the bar after a softball game, and now they are going to sing karaoke. They are all white, apparently middle class, and one of the men is carrying a baby in a blue sling across his chest. The song that they have chosen to sing is 'Gin and Juice,' a song written and made famous by rapper Snoop Dogg. The four softball players share two microphones between them. They sing the chorus, 'Rollin' down the street/Smokin' indo/Sippin' on gin and juice/Laid back/With my mind on my money and my money on my mind.' As they rap, the man farthest to stage right uses both of his hands to 'scratch' an invisible record player. The two women in the center of the group begin to flash 'gang signs,' or rather they provide a white, suburban parody of what they imagine are gang signs. Near the finale of the song, the man with the baby reaches down and grabs his own crotch with the hand that is not holding the baby. As the song ends, the quartet heads back to their table, giving each other 'high fives' and laughing loudly among themselves at their interpretation of the song.

While the group appears to be self-congratulatory and they are having a great time, every time I saw this kind of ironic performance of identity, it made me question the sincerity of the performers. The performance of these kinds of songs in such a mocking fashion always made me think of the history of minstrelsy, the Vaudevillian performance form that featured white people making fun of black people, complete with painted on blackface. To give them the benefit of the doubt, I am pretty sure that many, if not most of the white people who performed rap songs in this style, were probably not aware that they were behaving in a racist manner, at least not consciously. However, even if the performers were not aware of the implications of their performance, it demonstrates the way that social constructions of race and ethnicity are inscribed into our social conscious (and social unconscious).

In the book *Race Rebels: Culture, Politics, and the Black Working Class* (1994), professor of history and Africana studies Robin D. G. Kelly discusses some of the social implications associated with 'gangsta rap.' He explains, 'For other consumers of gangsta rap, such as middle-class white males, the genre unintentionally serves the same role as blaxploitation films of the 1970s or, for that matter, gangster films of any generation. It attracts listeners for whom the "ghetto" is a place of adventure, unbridled violence, erotic fantasy, and/or an imaginary alternative to suburban boredom' (Kelly 1994: 191). When viewed from this perspective, this example of white, middle-class suburbanites singing rap music can only be seen as derogatory, even if unintentional.

In this case, we see a negative construction of ethnicity performed from the outside in (versus a more organic construction of ethnicity that is performed from within a culture). Here, ethnicity is enacted as a performed boundary, composed of markers of identity that originate from both the outside and the inside of a specific group of people. This performed boundary marks who is included in the 'in-group' and who is included in the 'out-group.' The message that is being created through the performance by the white rappers comes through loud and clear: 'This is *not us*.'

I witnessed similar examples of ethnic performance at Capone's on a regular basis. There are only a few rap songs on the 'menu' at Capone's. Oddly enough, although there are many African Americans that frequent Capone's, I have only seen rap songs performed there by white people. This was one of the most unexpected phenomena that I encountered in my ethnographic research. When I started, I wondered whether people performed their identities when doing karaoke. For example, I wondered whether people would more commonly sing songs made famous by members of their own ethnic group. What I found was almost entirely the opposite.

Many times, I witnessed people singing who appeared to be African American, Latino/Latina, and Asian American. Contrary to what I expected, these individuals seemed to be just as likely to sing songs made famous by white people as they were to sing songs made famous by people of color. There were, of course, many times when I observed white people singing songs made famous by white people, which was the most likely scenario because the majority of the patrons at Capone's were white and the majority of the songs available were by white artists. However, I did occasionally observe patrons who were African American sing songs made famous by black artists; but in almost every case these were not rap songs, they were soul or R&B. Yet, almost every time that I observed someone sing a rap song, such as 'Baby Got Back,' by Sir Mix-a-Lot or 'Nuthin' but a "G" Thang,' by Dr. Dre, it was inevitably performed by white people.

Performing Authenticity

One can better understand this phenomenon by briefly looking at the history of popular music in the United States. In particular, I am interested in the concept of authenticity as it relates to ethnicity in the performance of music. At its core, the idea of 'authenticity' is problematic. In *Ethnicity, Identity and Music*, Martin Stokes writes, 'Clearly, notions of authenticity and identity are closely interlinked. What one is (or wants to be) cannot be "inauthentic," whatever else it is. Authenticity is definitely not a property of music, musicians and their relations to an audience. It is not even a Benjaminesque "aura" of uniqueness that surrounds a live situation as opposed to mechanically reproduced music. […] Instead, we should see "authenticity" is a discursive trope of great persuasive power' (Stokes 1994: 6–7). While there may be no such 'real' thing as 'authenticity,' if it can be understood as a discursive trope, then perhaps one can speak in terms of 'performances of authenticity.'

The implication of framing 'authenticity' as a performance points out that notions of the authentic and inauthentic are merely constructions. Although authenticity does not 'exist' in the real world, performances of authenticity do.

A working definition of authenticity is given by Simon Frith in his book *Performing Rites: On the Value of Popular Music*:

> First, *authenticity*. This clearly relates to questions of production but not to a thought-through theory; 'inauthentic,' that is to say, is a term that can be applied evaluatively even within genres which are, in production terms, 'inauthentic' by definition – fans can distinguish between authentic and inauthentic Eurodisco, and what is being described by implication is not how something was actually produced but a more inchoate feature of the music itself, a perceived quality of sincerity and commitment.
>
> (Frith 1996: 71, emphasis in original)

In the example of the white rappers, one would be hard-pressed to describe their performance of ethnicity as sincere. Although, in their own minds, the performance may not have been intended to reinforce stereotypes toward African Americans, I do not believe that the performers sincerely believed that they were performing an 'authentic' version of ethnicity. Could one, then, call this a performance of 'inauthenticity'?

Frith's attempt to link authenticity and sincerity reminds me of Erving Goffman's discussion of 'belief in the part one is playing' in *The Presentation of Self and Everyday Life* (1959). Goffman attempts to categorize performances into a binary model of the 'sincere' versus the 'cynical':

> At one extreme, one finds that the performer can be fully taken in by his own act; he can be sincerely convinced that the impression of reality which he stages is the real reality. [...] At the other extreme, we find that the performer may not be taken in at all by his own routine. [...] When the individual has no belief in his own act and no ultimate concern with the beliefs of his audience, we may call him cynical, reserving the term 'sincere' for individuals who believe in the impression fostered by their own performance.
>
> (Goffman 1959: 17–18)

Interestingly, Frith's concept of 'authenticity' and 'inauthenticity,' and Goffman's concept of the 'sincere' and the 'cynical,' parallel what karaoke ethnographer Robert Drew (2005) calls 'mimetic' versus 'ironic' performance styles. Borrowing from each, then, perhaps instead of talking about 'authentic' versus 'inauthentic' performances, one could differentiate the 'sincere' from the 'ironic.'

Consider Philip Auslander's discussion of authenticity in the book *Liveness: Performance in a Mediatized Culture* (1999). For Auslander, the function of live performance in the context of popular music is 'establishing the *authenticity* of the music for the rock fan' (Auslander 1999: 65, emphasis in original). Auslander goes on to discuss the work of

Theodore Gracyk (1996), who sees authenticity in rock as a 'romantic,' 'imaginary' concept. Auslander expands, 'Taken on its own terms, rock authenticity is an essentialist concept. [...] In my own discourse, however, I treat rock authenticity as an *ideological* concept and as a discursive effect' (Auslander 1999: 70, emphasis in original). Auslander's recognition that authenticity, while 'imaginary,' is treated as a 'real' thing in the world of rock fandom echoes Stokes' discussion of authenticity as a discursive trope.

Auslander elaborates on the concept of authenticity in his book *Performing Glam Rock: Gender and Theatricality in Popular Music* (2006). Although this book is primarily about the performance of gender, there are some cases where the subject of authenticity is analyzed in conjunction with the subject of ethnicity. Specifically, I want to explore a parallel between Auslander's discussion of the performance of gender and his discussion of the performance of ethnicity. One section of the book *Glam Rock* was originally published in 2003 as the article 'Good Old Rock and Roll: Performing the 1950s in the 1970s,' published in the *Journal of Popular Music Studies.* According to Auslander, borrowing the term from Grossberg (1992, 1993), Sha Na Na is an example of the performance of 'inauthenticity.'

In the case of the members of Sha Na Na, performers of many different ethnicities, including Irish and Jewish, took on different personas and used Italian names like 'Tony Santini,' 'Ronzoni,' and 'Gino.' Auslander explains, 'Sha Na Na's greaser look refers neither to the performance practices associated with the music they perform nor to the typical appearance of its audiences but, rather, to a stereotypical "Italian-Americanicity"' (Auslander 2003: 170). Auslander is referring to Roland Barthes' concept of 'Italianicity.' In *Image/Music/Text* (1977), Barthes writes about a visual image from an advertisement for Panzani brand Italian food used in a French marketing campaign. He comments about the way that the image evokes an imaginary sense of 'Italianicity' in the viewer, who is presumably French: 'The knowledge it draws upon is already more particular; it is a specifically "French" knowledge (an Italian would barely perceive the connotation of the name, no more probably than he would the Italianicity of tomato and pepper), based on a familiarity with certain tourist stereotypes' (Barthes 1977: 34).

Thus, Sha Na Na is an example of Italian-Americanicity because the performers are not actually Italian American, they are only approximating an image of the average American's stereotypes toward what is 'Italian.' Auslander considers Sha Na Na as an example of postmodernism because their performance style is based on irony. Their performance is reflexive, calling attention to itself as a construction. This brings us back to the example of the white rappers. If the performance of Sha Na Na can be considered as an example of 'Italian-Americanicity,' perhaps the performance of the softball players can be considered a performance of 'African-Americanicity.' The semiotics of both Barthes' food advertisement and the performance of the white rappers are based on stereotypes. Both Sha Na Na and the white rappers performed with an 'inauthentic' style based on irony. In these examples, the ironic performance style is used for the purposes of cultural boundary marking. Whether it is intentional or not, the ironic performance of the white rappers marks an ethnic boundary line.

Subverting Race

Numerous scholars have attempted to solve the various problems that have arisen from discussions of race within the field of popular music studies. Some scholars, such as Frith and Grossberg, have suggested that performances can be seen as existing on a spectrum somewhere between 'authenticity' and 'inauthenticity.' Auslander has argued that authenticity is a problematic concept embedded in the illusive notion of liveness, yet has 'real' power for the rock fan, and is best seen as an ideological, discursive concept. Goffman attempts to make a differentiation between performances that are 'sincere' and performances that are 'cynical.' In his work on karaoke, Drew has discussed styles of karaoke performance ranging from the 'mimetic' to the 'ironic.'

In this study, an attempt to use any of these approaches has proved to be problematic, for a variety of reasons. In the case of Timmy, one is tempted to equate a 'sincere' performance with an 'authentic' performance of ethnicity. However, in the example of Guns, we see that a 'sincere' performance does not necessarily equate with an 'authentic' performance at all. One also might be tempted to differentiate between 'authentic' and 'inauthentic' performances of identity using a litmus test of whether the performance is 'sincere' or 'ironic.' In the case of the 'white rappers,' we see how a performance that is probably sincere, at least from the point of view of the performers, can be interpreted as ironic when seen from the point of view of the audience. Ultimately, the Gordian Knot that has been tied between authenticity and ethnicity may never be untangled.

In fact, this analysis of the construction of ethnicity within performances of karaoke shows that notions of 'authentic' ethnicity are inherently problematic. I suggest that the reason for this conundrum lies in the fact that ethnicity and race are created by cultural, and not biological, factors. If race were truly the result of biological circumstances, then one would expect to be able to easily tell the difference between 'authentic' and 'inauthentic' ethnicities. The fact that these categories are not so easily discernable suggests that these categories have become 'naturalized' by cultural forces that have an interest in maintaining perceived racial differences for political purposes related to the maintenance of the hegemonic power structures embedded in the status quo. Thus, we once again see how performances of karaoke can subvert traditional categories of identity – in this case – ethnicity.

Regardless of the words that we use to describe these forces, one can see that the construction of ethnicity (as well as other categories of identity) takes place through the enactment of imaginary cultural boundaries, forged through microcosmic performances that happen all around us in everyday life. This idea of ethnicity as a performed boundary could also be applied to other categories of identity, such as gender and economic class, in addition to ethnicity. Ultimately, these categories of identity are all constructed through a delicate play between the ways that individuals identify themselves and the ways that other members of society identify them. Ultimately, labels such as 'gender,' 'ethnicity,' and 'class' are just that – labels. These labels are the markers of identity.

Yet, the fact that they are labels does not make them any less viable as powerful social agents. Performance of these labels gives them social force. That is, the performance of identities – of which the performance of gender, the performance of ethnicity, and the performance of class are examples – forms the basis of meaningful interactions between the individual and the society. The result is the very construction of culture. This playful dance between the roles and expectations that a community holds of an individual, and the roles and expectations that individuals hold of themselves is perhaps nowhere as much apparent as it is in the case of ethnicity. In the end, the fact that ethnicity is constituted through performance shows that ethnicity is entirely a cultural, rather than biological, phenomenon.

Chapter 5

Friends in Low Places

Blame it all on my roots,
I showed up in boots,
and ruined your black tie affair.

– Garth Brooks

Tex is a very large man. He probably weighs about 300 pounds. I have never seen him sing without wearing his large, black cowboy hat and his shiny, black cowboy boots. He is wearing a black-and-white, checkered long-sleeved shirt, cut and stitched western style at the neck and cuffs. The crowd listens to the first few bars of his rendition of 'Folsom Prison Blues' by Johnny Cash (based on 'Crescent City Blues' by Gordon Jenkins). Tex takes the stage, and picks up the microphone from its stand with his right hand. He sings, with a slight southern drawl, 'I hear the train a comin'/A comin' round the bend/I ain't seen the sunshine/Since I don't know when.' Almost as soon as he opens his mouth to sing the first words of the first verse of the song, I cannot help but think about a television commercial from over a decade ago that used the same melody. Only it went, 'I hear them trucks a comin'/A comin' round the bend/I ain't seen so many trucks/Since I don't know when.' The fact that suddenly I am reminded of trucks in the middle of a karaoke performance is a bit jarring, and makes me think about the very large role that economics and the flow of commerce plays in the context of a karaoke bar.

Another very interesting thing about this performance is the way Tex's persona plays into stereotypes about a certain class of people, the class of people who buy trucks. For decades, truck commercials in the United States have featured stereotypical images of working-class men, hauling various payloads of materials as part of their blue-collar jobs. Often the urban, 'working-class' stereotype bleeds into the rural, 'cowboy' stereotype. Tex is a living, breathing archetype of an image from one of these commercials. I am reminded of Jean Baudrillard's notion of contemporary culture as a simulation (see Baudrillard 1994). Is the image I see of Tex singing karaoke a reflection of the media's image of class or is the media's image of class a reflection of people like Tex who sing karaoke?

The materialization of the stereotype is also brought about by the fact that Tex chooses to sing this particular Johnny Cash song, the subject of which is a working-class man who is in prison. The coupling of this stereotypical image with this particular song resonates in a way that reminds me about how auto companies develop and market specific products to specific classes of people. Trucks are most heavily marketed toward working-class men. I have no idea what economic class Tex is actually from. For all I know, he could be an 'urban cowboy' who commands a six-figure salary at his office job at a bank, but I am prepared to wager that Tex's performance of his persona is 'authentic,' or at the very least, 'sincere.'

The Karaoke Dream

In the early evening, Capone's is a family restaurant, and the crowd is very different from the regular bar customers who begin to straggle in around nine o'clock when the karaoke singing starts. As the dining customers pay their bills and go home, different kinds of customers begin to take over different areas of the bar. There are at least two kinds of 'regular' customers: the regular karaoke singers and the non-singers. The regular karaoke singers like to sit at the central, long table that is directly across from the karaoke stage. The other regular customers are the ones who do not sing, and they usually stake out the row of stools at the end of the bar farthest from the stage.

Roger is an exception. He is one of the few barstool regulars who likes to sing karaoke. In full 'biker' gear, he approaches the microphone. He wears a black leather vest emblazoned with a Bald Eagle and the phrase 'Live to Ride,' a black baseball cap with an American flag on it, and black leather chaps, complete with a silver chain connecting the wallet in his pocket to his belt. He begins to sing the song 'Blue Jean Blues,' by ZZ Top. Roger seems to be very nervous and holds his body stiffly. He begins to sing softly and hesitantly; this may be the very first time he has ever sung karaoke. The lyrics to the song are simple and short, perhaps the reason why he may have picked this song. Roger stammers, 'I done ran into my baby/I fin'lly found my old blue jean/Well, I could tell that they was mine/From the oil and the gasoline.' As he finishes the song, he is met with a warm round of applause, with the loudest cheers coming from the section of the bar that usually does not participate in the karaoke. I will later find out that Roger is a blue-collar worker, a heavy machinery operator.

I witness Roger's rendition of 'Blue Jean Blues' near the beginning of my study. A week after this, I see him perform another ZZ Top song, 'Sharp Dressed Man,' again in his biker gear. Over the two years of my study, I observe Roger continue to sing and improve. Soon, he abandons his ZZ Top rock songs and begins to sing ballads. 'Mostly I sing Frank Sinatra,' he tells me, 'I liked Sinatra since I was a little kid. He was my hero.' I watch Roger transform from a nervous, novice singer into a captivating crooner. Interestingly, about the time that he switches genres, he also switches the clothing that he wears to the bar to sing karaoke, abandoning the leather biker gear for simple work shirts and blue jeans. Roger has a dream that is not uncommon among karaoke regulars. I often think of this as the 'Karaoke Dream,' the fantasy that one will be 'discovered' singing karaoke and go on to make their mark on the 'big time' entertainment industry.

Roger's dream is even more specific. He wants to be a lounge singer in Las Vegas. On another occasion, one of the regular singers tells me that Roger and he are going to go to another karaoke bar where the bartender 'has connections' in Las Vegas. Roger is hoping to make an impression and find out how he could become a lounge singer there. He even had someone record some of his karaoke performances, and had a 'demo' CD of the recordings created for him, complete with his picture on the cover. Roger informs me that he is going to send out some CDs to various agents and producers in Las Vegas as a sort of last-ditch effort to become famous before he goes off to Iraq. He explains to me, 'I recently got laid off, but I'm going to go to Iraq as a contractor about a month from now. I'm going to drive trucks around Baghdad. I have a bunch of these CDs that I'm going to send off to some people in Vegas before I go. Probably nothing will happen, but you never know.'

Roger's dream, the Karaoke Dream, is the dream of upward mobility through celebrity. Although there are many reasons why people sing, one of the most common reasons people give for singing is that it makes them feel like a celebrity. The pursuit of this desire can sometimes lead to economic exploitation. I have heard that there are people who unscrupulously prey on singers at karaoke bars, telling them that they are agents and duping them into paying them money to promote them, even though they are not very good singers. The Karaoke Dream is also capitalized on economically by every bar and restaurant that produces performances of karaoke. These businesses make money from karaoke nights, and thus capitalize on the desire of people to become rich and famous. Even beyond the world of karaoke, the dream of celebrity and upward mobility resonates in the consciousness of the contemporary consumer. One of the most prevalent tropes of the American mythos for the past century has been the 'Horatio Alger' figure, the poor man who pulls himself up by the bootstraps to become rich. The fantasy of becoming a star through the performance of karaoke is an extension of this myth. The Karaoke Dream is the new American Dream.

Ethnographer Rob Drew often talks about this subject: the extent to which the desire to be a celebrity has become ubiquitous in American society. Drew notes that:

> The precise meaning of the karaoke-as-stardom equation is often unclear, in part because the meaning of stardom itself is so elusive. Sometimes it seems only to refer to the outer trappings of stardom; the background music, the guaranteed applause, the microphones and spotlights are said to substantiate fantasies we've harbored since childhood when we hopped around our bedrooms and crooned into curling irons.
>
> (Drew 2001: 13–14)

Sometimes, the trope of stardom is used outside of the context of performance to include other aspects of everyday life. Drew observes:

> The language of celebrity gnaws its way under the skin of our most familiar rituals; stardom becomes a trope for any sort of public life or agency. [...] These days we scarcely notice our anonymity, our smallness of voice. We notice its absence, which we call stardom.
>
> (Drew 2001: 15)

Drew suggests that the dream to become famous is so widespread in our culture because people generally lack agency in their everyday lives. In this way, karaoke becomes a way for people to enact their agency. Performing karaoke is one of the few ways that the average person can 'act out' in public. Karaoke provides a public space where individuals are given free license to take hold of a microphone and broadcast their performances to an audience, thereby giving themselves a voice.

Highbrow/Lowbrow

In the book *Highbrow/Lowbrow: The Emergence of Cultural Hierarchy in America* (1988), Lawrence Levine discusses the ways the upper and lower classes became more stratified in America around the turn of the twentieth century. Levine argues that one of the results of establishing a status order was that once members of society had obtained a high degree of class privilege, they then began to 'attempt to hinder the free development of the market; to withhold certain goods from free exchange by monopolization' (Levine 1988: 230). He goes on to explain how the establishment of a new status order at the turn of the century affected the way that art was produced and consumed in America:

> The taste that now prevailed was that of one segment of the social and economic spectrum which convinced itself and the nation at large that its way of seeing, understanding, and appreciating music, theatre, and art was the only legitimate one; that *this* was the way Shakespeare, Beethoven, and Greek sculpture were meant to be experienced and in fact *had* been experienced always by those of culture and discernment. The accomplishment of the patrons of culture at the turn of the century was not only that they were now able to experience the expressive culture they appreciated, performed, and presented in ways they thought proper, but that everyone had to experience them in these ways as well. They became both the promoters and the arbiters of this corner of the cultural world and gradually appropriated the word 'culture' itself, which in popular parlance came more and more to signify the high arts.
>
> (Levine 1988: 231, emphasis in original)

In the case of karaoke, lower-class members of society become consumers of the dream of achieving the status afforded to members of the upper class. Thus, the economic exploitation of the dream of upward mobility depends upon this rift between the upper and lower classes, and the monopolization of the production of culture by a small group of people. The fact is, for most people, the dream of upward mobility is only a dream. Thus, the Karaoke Dream is made even more appealing to the masses because of the monopoly that the upper class holds over the production of culture.

The Karaoke Dream is also a dream of revolution. The performance of karaoke is squarely rooted in the so-called 'lowbrow' popular culture, and the stranglehold on cultural production is held by upper-class practitioners of 'highbrow' culture. Thus, the desire to be upwardly mobile through the performance of karaoke is a fantasy of revolution, the desire to knock down the barriers that divide the high and the low. Karaoke undermines class divisions because it challenges the boundary between 'high' and 'low' art. Karaoke is ultimately democratic because it allows all members of society equal access to a cultural space that is usually not available to the members of all classes. That is, karaoke as a platform for communication allows everyone to have a voice, regardless of actual social class, thus subverting the status order. This achievement may seem like a minor victory, hardly a challenge to the establishment. A conservative social critic may even dismiss the performance of karaoke as only an illusion of subversion, but the fact remains that the American view of the production of culture is quickly being transformed.

Rob Drew's karaoke ethnography was written many years ago, but at that time the tendency for Americans to be regarded as passive consumers was still widespread. Drew explains:

> Every attempt to extend music making runs up against the widespread belief that 'musicality' is an innate gift that some people have and others don't. [...] For many people, 'I can't sing' becomes an unproblematic description of a physical handicap – no different from 'I'm nearsighted' or 'I have a trick knee.'
>
> (Drew 2001: 33)

These beliefs are perpetuated through the typical excuses that people use to refuse to sing at karaoke bars. During my study, I often heard someone say, simply, 'I can't sing,' or 'Trust me, you don't want to hear me sing.' Tom, the Saturday night KJ at Capone's, tells me in one of the interviews, 'Some people are afraid to sing. They'll come up with all kinds of excuses. I teach singing, and before a recital my students will come down with a 104 degree fever, or their mother got hurt, or all kinds of things.' Drew explains how this widely held belief that one is 'unmusical' comes about:

> Such self-appraisals often can be traced to early childhood experiences: a grade-school music teacher's offhand insult, a failed bid for the glee club. The prescription such people internalize is *not* to sing, *not* to make music – at least not publicly – thus rounding out a cycle that assures their 'unmusicality.'
>
> (Drew 2001: 33, emphasis in original)

Yet today, years after Drew was writing, Americans seem to be becoming more and more likely to participate in public demonstrations of musical performance.

Brian Raftery explains how the performance of karaoke eventually became 'de-weirded' in his recent book, *Don't Stop Believin': How Karaoke Conquered the World and Changed My Life*: 'The combination of *American Idol, Lost in Translation*, and the teen-pop movement may have provided the country with a permission slip to sing' (Raftery 2008: 43). The chances of an average American participating in an amateur musical performance has been made even more likely by the sudden rise in popularity of interactive video games such as *Rock Band*, *Guitar Hero*, and *Karaoke Revolution*. A similar trend can be seen in the new media, in the movement from Web 1.0 to Web 2.0, a place where consumers become the producers of content on social media websites such as Facebook and Twitter.

The term 'Web 2.0' was coined by entrepreneur Tim O'Reilly, born out of an Internet conference brainstorming session (see O'Reilly 2005). O'Reilly and VP Dale Dougherty were discussing the aftermath of the bursting of the dot-com bubble in 2001. They noticed that companies that had survived the dot-com 'crash,' such as *Google*, *Yahoo!*, *Amazon*, and *eBay*, had several things in common. For example, these companies concentrated on delivering services rather than software. New advertising models concentrated on a grassroots, bottom-up model driven through the participation of consumers rather than a top-down model of publishing dictated by advertisers. These companies began to harness the collective intelligence of millions of users, growing their sites in response to user activity. Moreover, these companies began to treat their users as codevelopers rather than static consumers.

In retrospect, anyone watching the rise of the popularity of karaoke in the 1980s and 1990s, trends in which 'amateur' performers took up the mantle to become the creators of creative content instead of just passive consumers, could have predicted similar shifts in the realm of computer technology. Ultimately, the Web 2.0 shift would have an unprecedented effect on business models and the world economy, as traditional 'brick and mortar' storefronts were replaced by the virtual shopping malls of the future. Today, the most successful companies are those whose customers have a stake in shaping the business.

This new generation of digital performance is encouraging a new generation of Americans to become active participants in performance rather than participating only as members of a traditional, more passive audience. Raftery hypothesizes:

> *Guitar Hero* approximates what it feels like to be a rock star – or rather, what we *think* it must feel like. But another reason for the game's success is that in the post-*Idol* era, musical talent has been reduced to a commodity. It's something that can be dissected, replicated, mass-manufactured, and ultimately consumed.
>
> (Raftery 2008: 41, emphasis in original)

Although I believe that Raftery is correct that Americans' attitudes toward musical talent are changing, I disagree with his contention that interactive video games reduce talent to a commodity. If anything, the performance of music by amateur musicians turns them into producers, or at least it turns them into a new kind of active consumer.

The trend for Americans to become more likely to perform music in public backs up the ideas of John Blacking, who believes that the performance of music is a universal human trait. In *How Musical is Man?* (1973), Blacking discusses his experiences with the Venda people of South Africa, and how his study of the Venda began to break down long-held prejudices that he held about the superiority of western classical music and the 'primitive' nature of African music. Blacking tells us that in Venda society, it is assumed that every member of the culture is musical, and is expected to take part in musical performance. He writes:

> Suppose I argue that, because there are some societies whose members are as competent in music as all people are in language, music may be a species-specific trait of man. Someone will almost certainly retort that evidence of a widespread distribution of listening and performing ability among the Venda and other apparently musical societies should not be compared with the limited distribution of musical ability in, say, England because the complexity of English music is such that only a few could master it. In other words, if English music were as elementary as Venda music, then of course the English would seem to be as universally musical as the Venda! The broader implication of this argument is that technological development brings about a degree of social exclusion: being a passive audience is the price that some must pay for membership in a superior society whose superiority is sustained by the exceptional ability of a chosen few. The technical level of what is defined as musicality is therefore raised, and some people must be branded as unmusical.
>
> (Blacking 1973: 34)

The growing popularity of karaoke in America seems to support Blacking's argument that all humans are inherently musical. The karaoke mantra is, 'anyone can do it.' It will be very interesting to see if this trend continues. Presumably, if more people take up karaoke performance, if the trend toward user-generated content on the Web continues, and if more and more people begin to see amateur musical performance as something more normal than it has been viewed in the past, then there may be broader implications of this movement in terms of how culture is produced and distributed. This may result in a general loosening of the stranglehold that members of higher economic class have held on the production of culture since the beginning of the twentieth century.

Performing Class

Closing time at Capone's is drawing near. Usually, at one o'clock in the morning, the Saturday night KJ, Tom, thanks the crowd for coming and begins to pack up his equipment. Tonight, however, karaoke will go on for a little bit longer. A woman in her early fifties named Jane approaches Tom and asks to sing. When he explains that he has closed down for the night, she begs, 'Please, please, I need to sing this song!' She reaches into her purse and produces a twenty-dollar bill and hands it to Tom, 'Please I need to say goodbye to my baby.' Tom relents and lets her sing one more song. She thanks him and picks up the microphone. She tells the audience, 'I'm sorry, I'm starting to tear up. I just drove thirty hours to get here to bring my baby to you good people of Colorado.' She gestures toward her teenage daughter in the audience. 'She's going off to college now. You people take good care of her.' The song that Jane has chosen to dedicate to her daughter is 'Fancy' by Bobby Gentry, performed in the style of the American country music singer Reba McIntire.

The lyrics tell the story of a young girl whose mother buys an elegant satin 'dancing dress' for her daughter, despite the fact that she doesn't have enough money to buy food or pay the rent. Before she turns her daughter out onto the street, she tells her that she needs to learn how to act like a 'lady' in order to attract a man that will take care of her. The daughter, who is the protagonist of the song, explains matter-of-factly, 'That was the last time I saw my mamma/The night I left that rickety shack/The welfare people came and took the baby/Mama died and I ain't been back.' But the character in the song does not despair. She pledges to remake herself, to become upwardly mobile through her charm, 'Then I made myself this solemn vow/That I's gonna to be a lady someday [...] I mighta been born just plain white trash/But Fancy was my name.' By the end of the song Fancy has made herself rich, explaining, 'I charmed a king, a congressman and an occasional aristocrat/Then I got me a Georgia mansion and an elegant New York townhouse flat.' The message of the song is multifaceted. It is a tale of upward mobility, the story of a woman who ascends the economic ladder by changing the way that she acts and the way that she dresses. That is, just like the character Eliza Doolittle in the musical *My Fair Lady*, she 'performs' her class.

In addition to the subjects raised by the narrative of the song itself, there is also an additional level of meaning added through the song's performance as karaoke. The song is framed within the context of a mother sending her daughter off to college. The semantics of this performance are also complicated by the parallel existence of a mother/daughter pair in the narrative of the song and a mother/daughter pair in the context of the karaoke performance. Jane's dedication of the song to her college-aged daughter in the audience invokes the metaphor of a mother who wants to see her daughter succeed in the world. The selection of this particular song also leads me to speculate that Jane and her daughter are probably from a family of modest means. Also, another parallel that occurs to me, and is probably another reason why Jane chooses this song, is how the expensive dress in the song is the analog of the expensive college education that Jane is giving her daughter. The resonance of Jane's story with the narrative of the song brings tears to my eyes. I am touched by the honesty of the song and the way that it is performed as a way to send a young woman off to college, with a dream of upward mobility.

The Dragon and the Pearl

Another very good example of the performance of economic class comes from Casey Lum's ethnography about karaoke, *In Search of a Voice* (1996), in which he writes about three different Asian American communities around the New York City and Northern New Jersey. One of the karaoke scenes that Lum describes is a private karaoke 'club' in an affluent neighborhood in New Jersey. In this kind of club, very common in many Asian American communities, members pay to join and then take turns hosting private parties where the singing of karaoke is the main attraction. Lum explains, 'These people, particularly club members, came mostly from Taiwan and have been in the United States for 20 to 30 years, [...] They are upper middle to upper class professionals working mostly for U.S. corporations or business owners. Coming from very comfortable backgrounds, many of these people have an annual income well in the six-figure range' (Lum 1996: 57). The fact that these parties are private is one of the ways class differentiation is marked, through the basic level of access: who is invited and who is uninvited. 'Private' is 'privilege.'

Lum takes his readers to one of these karaoke parties, at a man named John's house. John got his medical degree in Taiwan, immigrated to the United States and now he works at a hospital in Manhattan. As a way to demonstrate his economic success to other members of his community, John had a 2,000 square-foot karaoke ballroom built in the basement of his 7,000 square-foot French provincial chateau in a quiet New Jersey suburb. When viewed from a dramaturgical standpoint, the performance of class in Lum's example takes place on three levels: the setting, the costumes, and the singing. The way that one dresses is one of the most obvious markers of economic class. Lum tells us at this party, 'The majority of the men were dressed semiformally in jacket and tie. The women were conspicuously more fashionable, all clad in expensive party dresses' (Lum 1996: 55). Thus, wearing expensive clothes is one of the more obvious ways a person performs their membership in the upper class through conspicuous consumption.

The most extravagant aspect of Lum's example is the setting, the architecture of the ballroom itself:

> It is acoustically designed, with numerous speakers installed at the top of the two long walls to beam sound to the solid wood dance floor at a 45-degree angle. One of the long walls is adorned by tall, mirrored panels that reflect the moving images of people entering or dancing in the ballroom. Part of the ceiling is also covered with mirrors to give people a view of the dance floor and themselves at an angle; the mirrors also reflect light from the mirrored ball hanging from the ceiling. [...] At one end of the ballroom is a stage equipped with a large-screen, front-projection television system. [...] Directly across the long dance floor from the stage is another mirrored wall. On it, there are a pair of large and vividly-carved dragons painted in stunning gold. The bulging eyes and fierce claws of the two dragons converge on a pearl.
>
> (Lum 1996: 66–67)

The amount of money that John must have spent to build this extravagant ballroom is conspicuously revealed to the partygoers through the pure spectacle of the scene. Lum explains that dragons in Chinese culture symbolize power and masculinity. Lum states, 'the artifact suggests a degree of self-reference – of supremacy, competitiveness, and wealth' (Lum 1996: 67). An additional level of meaning in this image comes from the association of dragons with masculinity. Lum interprets the iconography further, 'The icon seems to suggest the conspicuous grace and force in the men's pursuit of, or fight for, the woman of their choice, something precious, or, simply, something worthy of being won' (Lum 1996: 67). Thus, the dragon emblem in the karaoke ballroom is another example of the ways performances of gender can become entangled in performances of economic class.

Another aspect of the performance of class at these parties is the way karaoke is sung. For the most part, only club members are allowed to perform, and performers must pay for membership in the club. This is an example of the enforcement of class boundaries through the exercise of exclusive access. In addition, most of the club members hire private vocal teachers to help them improve their singing. The order of singers for the evening is fixed beforehand, and a program listing the order of the singers is printed out and distributed to the audience before the evening begins. In these ways, the performances of singers at John's party are atypical of the average karaoke singer in the United States. The spirit here is much more competitive than in the typical public karaoke bar, where all singers are given encouragement and are judged more leniently by the audience, regardless of their ability. Thus, the nature of the singing itself is another way that the performance of economic class infiltrates the scene. Together, the specific meanings that are produced by the extravagant setting, the expensive costumes, and the competitive singing style provide us with another excellent example of the performance of economic class.

Subverting Class

Rich and Sally are regulars at Capone's. Rich has been coming here for eight years. Sally met Rich here, and they have been dating for about a year now. Rich is a car salesman in a neighboring suburb. He tells me that sales are slow right now, especially because the state of the economy has slowed down the automobile industry. Sally is a single mother and works part-time for a local man who used to own a CD store, but now sells CDs on the Internet out of his basement. Even though times are tough, they still have enough money to come to Capone's, order pitchers of beer, and participate in karaoke nights.

Sally does not usually sing, but she comes to karaoke for the community it provides and to watch the karaoke singers. One night near the end of my two-year study, Sally finally gets to fulfill one of her Karaoke Dreams, which is, oddly, to sing the children's song 'I'm a Little Teapot.' Even though it is on the list of available karaoke songs, the first time that she requested the song she was turned down by the Saturday night KJ. When she finally performs the song it is unspectacular. The song is only about thirty seconds long, and she stands about five feet away from the microphone, singing at such a low level that we can hardly hear her. It is a shame that her performance is not more proficient. Her choice of this particular song reminds me of some of the ironic, self-reflexive performances of the late comedian Andy Kaufman. Just as Kaufman defied the expectations of his audience by playing 'The Mickey

Mouse Theme' on a portable record player or singing 'One Hundred Bottles of Beer' instead of performing standard stand-up comedy, Sally defies the expectations of her audience by singing a children's song instead of performing standard karaoke fare.

Some of the most memorable performances of karaoke that I see during my study are by Rich. What differentiates him from the average karaoke performer is that sometimes he sings wearing various costumes. He explains, 'My friend and I used to come here in costume to break the ice. We were both new in town, and it was a way to meet people.' In the past I witnessed Rich sing wearing a 'pirate' costume and a 'pimp' costume. Tonight he is wearing overalls with no shirt underneath, a straw hat, leather sandals, and he has a long piece of hay in his mouth. Rich chooses the song 'I Touch Myself' by the Divinyls. Rich drifts between singing the actual lyrics of the song and a kind of stream-of-consciousness, improvisational rant.

Rich's costumed and improvised performances are a good example of what Rob Drew calls an 'ironic' performance style (versus a purely 'mimetic' performance style). Drew's discussion of the topic is focused on the issue as it relates to class, and can be found in his 2005 article, '"Once More With Irony": Karaoke and Social Class.' In it, Drew contends that during the late 1990s, the ironic style of performing karaoke became popular with members of the middle- and upper-middle class. He explains:

> Karaoke seemed only to be adopted on the condition that no one took it seriously. Performers at such bars would sing with exaggerated and obviously insincere feeling, or they would sing in inappropriate styles (for instance, singing a ballad in a hard rock voice), or adopt comic voices, or sing parodic lyrics, or (the simplest and commonest option) they would simply flood out with laughter throughout their performances.
>
> (Drew 2005: 376)

Drew turns to theories regarding popular culture by Pierre Bourdieu and Herbert Gans to explain the phenomenon of ironic performance styles among middle- and upper-middle-class performers:

> My understanding of class is based in what Gans (1974) defines as 'taste cultures' or what Bourdieu (1984) defines as 'habitus.' Urban bohemia is defined not only by traditional class markers such as individual and family wealth, education, and occupation, but by preferences for particular cultural objects.
>
> (Drew 2005: 372–373)

In this case, the cultural object in question is the performance of karaoke. Drew's argument rests on the assumption that during the early period of its history in America, primarily during the 1980s, karaoke was particularly appealing to the working-class taste culture.

Drew hypothesizes that the rise of the ironic mode of performance during the 1990s coincides with the rise in its popularity among middle- and upper-middle-class performers.

Drew proposes that the ironic performance style is a kind of 'boundary marking' of economic class:

> The object of humor was the persona of 'karaoke performer' itself, the very act of karaoke performance. [...] What is it about the practice of karaoke that incurs middle-class performers' ridicule? I've already alluded to one factor: cultural boundary marking. The very fact that it is a popular working- and lower-middle-class practice often marks karaoke as alien for middle-class observers. The ironic stance toward performance thus allows certain middle-class performers to participate in karaoke while still maintaining a sense of class distinction and superiority.
>
> (Drew 2005: 378)

Drew's assertion that the ironic style of performing karaoke is a cultural marker of identity flies in the face of critics, such as Diana Crane, John Seabrook, and David Brooks, who contend that cultural boundaries have become blurred because of the advent of the mass media.

Crane theorizes in her book *The Production of Culture: Media and the Urban Arts*, 'It is necessary to replace the outmoded terms *high culture* and *popular culture*. It is more useful to think in terms of culture produced by national culture industries and culture produced in urban subcultures, including various art worlds and ethnic subcultures' (Crane 1992: 9, emphasis in original). Seabrook calls the new, intermingled class that results from the effects of national culture industries 'nobrow' culture (see Seabrook 2001). Brooks calls it the 'bourgeois bohemian' class, or 'bobo' for short (see Brooks 2000). Drew explains:

> Seabrook's nobrow blurs taste categories and is defined in particular by its embrace of commercial culture [...] David Brooks coins the term 'bobo' (or 'bourgeois bohemian') to define an urban middle class that, in his view, confounds the old divisions between holders of economic, educational, and cultural capital [...] Brooks claims that this new 'bobo' class further confuses class definitions by practicing 'one-downsmanship,' that is, taking on the trappings of the working and the lower classes.
>
> (Drew 2005: 373)

Drew, however, suggests that the popularity of the ironic mode of performance among middle- and upper-middle-class performers is evidence of an enduring division between the classes. He contends, 'The laughter of karaoke can be taken as what card sharps call a "tell"; it betrays not only the performer's class, but the enduring class divisions within this putatively "nobrow" cultural form' (Drew 2005: 381).

Drew's contention that the ironic mode of performance is primarily connected to class division is very convincing. On the one hand, the ironic performance style is certainly sometimes used as a kind of cultural boundary marker. On the other hand, the connection between the ironic mode of performance and the performance of social class is not as clear as Drew makes it out to be. As an example of how the ironic performance style is not always about the blurring of class lines, remember the examples of Rich and Sally. Neither Rich nor Sally is by any means upper class. They tell me, like many of us, that they often struggle from week-to-week to pay their bills and make a living. In the case of Rich and Sally, and because I have known them for some time, I would guess that their ironic performance styles may be more a reflection of their personalities than their economic class. Or, the ironic performance style may be due to another factor: age. Younger generations of Americans have been brought up on the irony of bands such as Nirvana and television shows such as *Jackass*.

Because of the vast shift in cultural values over the years, the ironic mode of performance can be used to mark generational boundaries as well. In addition, Rich's costuming choices of wearing overalls with no shirt, a straw hat, and a sprig of hay in his mouth alludes to another kind of cultural boundary marking, drawing the line between rural and urban members of the working class. Given the context of the performance is karaoke night at Capone's, and knowing that country music is the most popular song choice, Rich's act could be interpreted as a comment directed toward some of the country singers at Capone's. Rich's performance points to the fact that he may be part of the urban working class, but, at least from his standpoint, that is better than being a member of the rural working class. Rich's performance also had a dimension related to the performance of gender because of his choice of singing a song about masturbation usually sung by a woman. The fact remains, however, that whether the ironic style is being used to mark the boundaries of ethnicity, class, gender, or other categories of identity, such as age or locality, these performances are nonetheless being performed to mark cultural boundaries of various kinds.

Liveness Anxiety

As a technology of the mass media, the performance of karaoke can be seen as both a contagion of and an anecdote for the postmodern condition. In 'Karaoke: Subjectivity, Play and Interactive Media,' Johan Fornäs states:

> A culturally conservative critic might see karaoke as yet another example of how we are voided by the profit-greed of popular culture industries, how personal authenticity is removed and replaced by insipid copies of idols. Here we learn to imitate Madonna and Michael Jackson to artificial melodies that approximate equally artificial pop ideals hatched in some distant multinational metropole. The music and the videos are empty simulations, lacking in soul, false fetiches for idolatry and submission to the dictates of fashion. [...] Behold, our ultimate colonization by the inauthenticity of mass culture!
> (Fornäs 1994: 95)

Robert Drew also discusses the way the singing of karaoke has been accused of being a pathogenic symptom of the disease of postmodernism: 'The conventional wisdom is that karaoke performers don't express much of anything, they merely sing other people's songs. [...] karaoke is nothing more than a simulacrum, one more symptom of the recession of reality in a post-modern age' (Drew 2001: 51). Negative reactions directed at karaoke (and many other forms of amateur performance) are common among social critics and members of the general public alike. Usually, though, these musings come from people who have never tried singing karaoke. In fact, I would argue, karaoke embraces the potential for cultural resistance against hegemonic tendencies.

I attribute this sort of fear of assimilation that accompanies the topic of karaoke to what I call 'liveness anxiety.' Liveness anxiety is characterized by attacks on the technological aspects of culture that threaten to replace live performance. Liveness anxiety is a particular kind of anxiety, one that goes well beyond traditional anti-theatricality or performance anxiety. With performance anxiety the fear that arises comes from inside the performer, while with liveness anxiety the fear arises from outside the performer, from the observer. Liveness anxiety is not the fear of performing, it is a territorial behavior that is common in social critics, scholars, and artists themselves; it is a fear of performances that depart from the standard template of acceptable cultural production as is dictated by hegemonic forces.

The concept of liveness is discussed in Philip Auslander's 1996 article 'Liveness: Performance and the Anxiety of Simulation,' and is expanded on at length in his book *Liveness: Performance in a Mediatized Culture*. For Auslander, the problem of liveness is associated with poststructuralist Jean Baudrillard's theory of simulation (see Baudrillard 1994). While many performance theorists continue to insist that there is a real binary relationship between the 'live' and the 'mediatized,' Baudrillard and Auslander see this binarism collapsing, actually imploding, in a contemporary society in which the media plays an ever-increasing role. Auslander states, 'In the case of live and mediatized performance, the result of implosion is that a seemingly secure opposition is now a site of anxiety, an anxiety that infects all who have an interest in maintaining the distinction between the live and the mediatized. It is manifest in some performance theorists' assertions of the integrity of the live and the corrupt, coopted nature of the mediatized' (Auslander 1996: 203). This same kind of anxiety is present at the site of karaoke performance. Moreover, I suggest that this 'liveness anxiety' is connected to economic class and desire by members of the intelligentsia to maintain the status quo and stranglehold on their control of the means of cultural production.

Consider some of the following quotes, collected from various articles from beat writers and music critics in the mainstream press. An article titled 'It's Time to Maim That Tune' ran in *Newsweek* in 1992, describing karaoke singers as 'No-Talents, making fools of themselves before complete strangers' (Newsweek Staff 1992: 57). A reporter for the *Indianapolis Star* called karaoke 'A strange subculture of regulars who meet at the same places every week to act out their Big Time Pop Star fantasies for each other' (Redmond 1998: E1). A promoter at a local bar that had to replace their live musicians with karaoke to cut costs in the struggling economy bemoaned, 'It's so anti-music, so anti-life' (Stoute 1995: H7).

To some degree, these anti-karaoke messages can be attributed to a general trend in American culture, the decline of membership in social organizations and the seeming disappearance of public life. Drew explains, 'This image of karaoke performance as a form of sociopathy is a sign of how anxiety ridden public interaction seems to have become in U.S. society. Participation in public forms of recreation has declined for decades, as has membership in civic, religious, and school-based organizations' (Drew 2001: 69). This general perception that interaction in public is on the way out is commonly attributed to the rise of electronic communication technologies such as the Internet, e-mail, and television. Thus, at first glance, karaoke seems to be just another example of an interactive technology that is going to cause detrimental harm to society.

Much of this anxiety also stems from a fear of technology that is particularly common in American culture. Take, for example, the large number of movies and television shows about a robot or computer that maliciously tries to take over the world. In the context of karaoke, the fear becomes directed toward the fact that karaoke seems to be a threat to live performers. Drew writes, 'The specter arises of karaoke *replacing* live entertainment. Like sound technologies from the microphone to the drum machine, karaoke gets accused of substituting the "direct" encounters of "real" musical performance with a body-snatcher inhumanity' (Drew 2001: 21, emphasis in original). In this context, liveness anxiety arises from a fear of mediatization, a fear that somehow the identities of both performer and audience will be stolen away, swept up in the torrent of bits that comprise the digitized part of the performance.

Auslander claims that, because members of our society are so heavily exposed to the media, live performance is losing its cultural significance. Auslander maintains, 'The primary experience of the music is as a recording; the function of live performance is to authenticate the sound on the recording' (Auslander 1999: 160). On the other hand, the simple 'live vs. canned' binarism on which Auslander's argument rests has itself been challenged. Performances of karaoke also problematize this seemingly simple relationship.

At first glance, karaoke seems to be just another example of how 'liveness' is being pushed out of our lives. Karaoke, as a technology of music replication, is often subject to the same kind of criticisms that have been directed toward artists who are part of the mainstream music industry. Consider the tendency for hardcore rock fans (and critics) to look down on musicians who play cover songs. This same attitude carries over to karaoke. In '"Scenes" Dimensions of Karaoke in the United States,' Drew writes, 'I've often found that "serious" rock fans react to it with the most disdain. Rock fans and musicians say it involves a high degree of technological mediation [...] consisting of "cover versions," which are traditionally subordinated in rock' (Drew 2004: 65). Of course, the notion that 'real' music does not involve technological mediation is a fallacy. The technology that allows for the performance of karaoke is the same technology that allows music to be recorded, distributed to consumers, and listened to by devotees.

I propose that the fear that surrounds karaoke, and other types of amateur performance (especially mediatized forms of amateur performance), can be attributed to 'liveness anxiety.' Liveness anxiety can also extend beyond the realm of amateur performance, and can become directed at any mediatized performance, regardless of the possible skill and virtuosity of the artist. Ultimately, the idea of liveness is a fetish. That is, it is a cultural object desired by individuals in an unnatural way. Because they see digital media as part of the establishment, many theater artists and scholars cling to the notion that liveness is the last viable platform from where it is possible to mount performances that challenge the status quo. Theater artists and social critics who maintain this belief are actually doing themselves a disservice. In reality, the liveness fetish is a tool of the capitalist system of cultural production. Auslander comments on the connection between liveness and the anxiety that is associated with the fear of its disappearance: 'Anxiety is also manifest in the response of capital to the collapse of this distinction. Simulation occurs at the moment a cultural economy is thoroughly saturated with repetitions. It threatens to undermine the economy of repetition by imploding oppositions on which that economy depends: in order to render performance in a repeatable form, there must be an "original" performance to reify' (Auslander 1996: 203).

Consider the previous discussion of the history of 'highbrow' and 'lowbrow' art in America. Lawrence Levine has proposed that the origins of high and low art are rooted in class differences. By the turn of the century, a small group of people from the upper class laid claim to 'culture.' By monopolizing cultural production, this group was able to maintain a grip on the social status that they had achieved. This shift depended on the claim that only a certain group of talented artists was good enough to create art. Thus, amateurs were pushed to the periphery and the means of cultural production was coopted by the elite. The result was the origin of what is now a widespread belief that the reason why people should not perform is that they do not have talent. Thus, the majority of people in American society have been branded as 'unmusical' or 'inartistic.' The result is the maintenance of the social order. The anxiety that surrounds the performance of karaoke can be seen as an extension of these ongoing biases.

When viewed in this way, the ontological claim to the efficacy of live performance can be seen as a power grab. Why should only live performers be allowed to change culture? This is the insidious underbelly of liveness anxiety. The biases against performances that are not 'live' perpetuate the division of cultural production, and maintain the position of theater as a primarily 'highbrow' art form. Ironically, these biases are perpetuated by the very same artists who are attempting to overcome the stranglehold of hegemony through their work. Unfortunately, the more we cling to the notion that liveness is a privileged domain of cultural production, the more we maintain the status quo. The harder we fight to maintain a claim on the value and meaning of live performance, the longer class divisions and the widespread view that theater is a trapping of the upper class will continue.

The good news is that the performance of karaoke may hold the answer to this problem. Ironically, the value of karaoke may lie in the fact that it is neither entirely canned nor entirely live. It is what Charles Keil calls the 'mediated and live' (see Keil 1994). Deborah

Wong writes about this idea in her 1994 article '"I Want the Microphone": Mass Mediation and Agency in Asian-American Popular Music,'

> Karaoke takes the very notions of live and canned and messes them up, rendering them ambiguous. Performance studies theorist Sharon Mazer suggests that we compare karaoke to the pleasures of watching puppet theater: the puppet, she says, 'makes manifest the distinction between alive and not alive because it verges on but never attains the status of "living."' Karaoke hinges on the fact that it's not *all* mediated, not canned – is, in fact, alive.
>
> (Mazer qtd. in Wong 1994: 164, emphasis in original)

One common objection to the value of karaoke performance that I have often encountered is the idea that karaoke is only an imitation, and therefore is not worthy of being considered as valuable as a purely live performance. I understand how someone who has never performed karaoke may agree with this idea. However, because I have been performing karaoke for a couple of years now, I can assure you that the performance of karaoke is not that simple. There were many times when I sang songs that I attempted to copy the original artist. This was my first approach to singing songs by The Cars, for example. I would attempt to emulate the voices of singers Benjamin Orr and Ric Ocasek, to varying degrees of success. Strangely, I found that the better I was at copying the original voice, the less people would listen to me singing. It was almost as if, at a certain point, they tuned out my singing because it might as well have been playing on the juke box, and they went back to their private conversations at their individual tables. I was much more successful and appreciated in my singing when I sang in my own voice and did not attempt to copy the original. I would get more applause, more high fives, and more laughter and excitement as I returned to the table when, as they say on *American Idol*: 'I make it my own.'

In the Introduction to the edited volume, *Performance, Culture, and Identity*, Elizabeth C. Fine and Jean Haskell Speer write:

> While there are certainly performances that are merely mimetic, in the Platonic sense, the best performances are mimetic in the Aristotelian sense. That is, they involve analysis and reflection. They condense the raw stuff of behavior to reveal essential and universal features. Thus, such performances involve poiesis – the art of making, as opposed to simple imitation. Performance, then, as poiesis, makes or constitutes cultural identity, as well as imitates it.
>
> (Fine and Speer 1992: 9)

Thus, I began to understand that the best karaoke performances are poetic, not mimetic.

As previously mentioned, the word 'kara' in karaoke is often translated as 'empty,' but literally it means 'void' (Mitsui 1998: 40). Johan Fornäs uses the metaphor of the 'void' to theorize about subjectivity. In many ways, the ideas of Fornäs bridge the gap between the modern and the postmodern. On one level, he follows Derrida (1978). Tōru Mitsui discusses this aspect of Fornäs' work in the introduction of *Karaoke Around the World*: 'His notion of a "disappearing act" or of "filling the gaps" in one's multiple identities is especially revealing' (Mitsui 1998: 15). Fornäs explains further, 'This interactive medium can serve as a paradigmatic model for how media texts always offer their users voids. Listeners, viewers and readers enter into these gaps and fill them with their own (re)constructed meanings' (Fornäs 1994: 97). Thus, it is this live aspect of singing within a performance of karaoke that fills the void created by the recorded background music.

Wong elaborates on Fornäs' idea of karaoke as a void. She writes, 'Karaoke presupposes and is structured around an empty space, a place meant to be filled by a live, not-canned person whose performance will merge with the package, a person who fills sonic and social and historical space, and whose performance becomes larger than life' (Wong 1994: 162). Although the background music of the karaoke performance is recorded, every performance of a karaoke song is essentially live because there is no way to tell beforehand exactly how the song will be sung, how the audience will react, or a number of other mitigating factors that arise because karaoke is performed in a public venue in the presence of a live audience.

Wong writes that the performance of karaoke can even be seen not as a symptom of postmodernism, but rather as a form of resistance against the mediatization. Wong writes:

> While mass mediation is often considered a hegemonic force, people can (and do) reclaim mass-mediated musics for their own purposes. I've seen how Southeast Asians constantly and enthusiastically put liveness back into genres that seem to epitomize the hegemonic evils of the transnational music industry.
>
> (Wong 1994: 155)

Thus, resistance only becomes possible because karaoke is part of the mass media. It attacks from within. Fornäs echoes a similar sentiment:

> We may fill the void in karaoke music with the voids in ourselves. Our voices may smoothly reflect the impersonal surface of the world around us, and perhaps the opportunity to do this is exactly what we need: to try out different masks, to test the fascination of artificiality. But we may also choose to sing with passion, off key and hoarsely, but full of our unique experience which no machine can take from us.
>
> (Fornäs 1994: 96)

Because it is already part of the system, karaoke is a viable location for mounting a defense against the onslaught of culture producers.

It is very tempting to dismiss karaoke as a passing fad. It is even more tempting to dismiss karaoke as a gimmick, a technological crutch that gives untalented people a false hope of celebrity. In fact, karaoke is not a fad. It is not going away any time soon. It is a multibillion dollar industry that continues to grow every year. I predict that we will see this trend continue.

Karaoke is also part of a larger cultural movement, along with video games such as *Rock Band* and *Guitar Hero* and social networking websites such as Facebook and Twitter, which promotes the average individual as a worthwhile producer of culture. This is why karaoke (and this trend in general) is truly revolutionary. It challenges the hegemonic forces of the status quo by breaking down the rules under which cultural production is understood to take place. The anxiety that surrounds its production is ultimately the strongest evidence of its efficacy. Karaoke provides the cultural space and environment where anyone, regardless of their gender, ethnicity, or class, can truly have a voice.

Chapter 6

Sweet Caroline

Hands, touchin' hands.
Reachin' out, touchin' me, touchin' you.

– Neil Diamond

Tonight is a typical Wednesday night at Capone's. Most of the regulars are here, including Ed. I have been sitting with him, reminiscing about his life. One of the things that I did not expect to happen during my study of karaoke is the way that I became good friends with many of the people I met. Ed is, in fact, one of the best friends that I have made during my time spent at Capone's. He is a fascinating man. He is a man in his eighties, one of the most gentle, kind souls I have ever met. He has been telling me about how he used to be a very rich man. According to his stories, he used to own houses on both coasts, a private jet, and had a collection of vintage cars. All of this changed when he was in a car accident. Ed spent years in a hospital bed. He describes to me the pain and agony he went through, the cascading failures of the different organs in his body, test after test that were ordered by his doctors, and the way that the costs of these events eventually whittled away his fortune. Ed had good health insurance, but eventually he reached the limits of his policy and had to dip into his own retirement funds to cover his care. Eventually, it drove him into bankruptcy. He was finally released from the hospital a few months ago. Since then, he has been coming to Capone's every week for karaoke night. Ed does not drink alcohol. I do not know if this has anything to do with his accident, and I do not ask. Instead, Ed orders diet Coca-Cola. Ed is single now. He sometimes talks about his wife, who passed away a few years ago. He never tells me the circumstances of her death. I instinctively feel that the topic is off limits. I get the feeling that he comes here for the company.

Tonight's KJ, Ron, comes over to our table to tell Ed it is his turn to sing. Ron hands the microphone to Ed. Ed, in turn, hands the microphone to me and asks me to hold it as he struggles to get up from his chair and puts his weight onto the cane that he uses for support. After he gets up, I hand the mike back to him and he slowly walks toward the stage. The first few notes of one of Ed's go-to songs play over the PA system. The song is 'Unchained Melody,' written by Alex North and Hy Zaret, as made famous by The Righteous Brothers. Ed closes his eyes as the first few halting notes roll by. I wonder what he is thinking about. Is he lost in nostalgia, envisioning people that he used to know and love? Or is he lost in the song? Ed starts to sing. He has the voice of an angel. He croons, 'Oh, my love, my darling,

I've hungered for your touch, a long, lonely time.' The emotion in his voice is palpable. A tear comes to my eye as I think about the stories that Ed has been telling me, and I wonder who it is in his memory that he is singing to. Is it his wife? Some other lost love? Or is it only the image of some imaginary paramour? He continues, 'Lonely rivers flow to the sea, to the sea, to the open arms of the sea/Lonely rivers sigh, "Wait for me, wait for me." I'll be coming home, wait for me!' For a moment, Ed's singing makes me wonder about my own life, and what I will be like when I am his age. Will I be lonely? Will I be with the one that I love? How will I feel about my own impending mortality? The finale of the song crescendos, and Ed leans into the high notes at the peak of the chorus, 'And time goes by so slowly, and time can do so much, are you still mine?/I need your love. I need your love. God speed your love to me!'

As the song comes to an end, the audience claps for Ed. He hands the microphone back to Ron, and slowly shuffles back to our table. He leans his cane next to his chair, and gives me a smile as he sits down. Everyone in the bar, including myself, has been through a gamut of emotions, lost in the melancholy of Ed's song. But despite the sadness that is in the air, I get the sense that this is what makes Ed happy these days. Ed is one of thousands upon thousands of people who find joy in singing karaoke. Performing on stage, sharing bits of ourselves and our own stories in song can help to make life more meaningful. Beyond the sometimes egocentric satisfaction that performing can bring, there is perhaps an even greater happiness found in the people you meet when you are waiting to go on stage. There are unspoken rules, shared etiquette, and understandings between karaoke singers. We depend on one another for support. In karaoke, the performance space is a judgment-free zone, no matter how good or how poor a singer might be. It is within the midst of this comradery, the mutual admiration and support that grows between karaoke singers, that friendships are made. A community is born.

The Evolution of Singing

The history of karaoke can be seen as the continuation of a thread that runs from prehistory to present times. The phenomenon of public singing has historically existed along a sort of continuum. At its point of origin, singing is a skill that may have begun as an evolutionary adaptation for survival. Anthropologists have tried to explain the universal appeal of music. Some have compared the human singing to mating calls in various species. Others suggest that singing is an essential element of social behavior in general, justifying their reasoning with what has been labeled 'call and response' theory. Call and response is defined by the sociologist Geneva Smitherman as 'spontaneous verbal and nonverbal interaction between speaker and listener in which all of the statements ("calls") are punctuated by expressions ("responses") from the listener' (Smitherman 1977: 104). Gonda attempts to explain the appeal of karaoke using call and response theory in his article, 'The Philosophy of Singing.' He states, 'One idea of the origin of singing concerns the theory of "call and response." It is theorized that tribes, clans and groups of peoples in long distant eras (cave-person times) did not possess language sophisticated enough to engage in interpersonal communication' (Gonda 1993: 30). Types of call and response might have included signals to announce the arrival of prey, the arrival of predators, or perhaps specific calls and responses to mark in-group/out-group distinctions among other groups of humans.

This makes a lot of sense, given the environment of early humans in the savannahs of Africa, where visibility was low and the need for survival was high. Biologists have observed singing behavior in diverse animal species from songbirds to gibbons. Today, chimpanzees and bonobos, for example, typically roam in groups of twenty to thirty (or sometimes more) individuals. Ape colonies have been observed to cooperatively hunt in small groups, and occasionally have been observed 'going to war' with neighboring groups over territory and/or access to females (see de Waal 1989). If it is true that these animals are our closest relatives, then the possibility that singing evolved as a way to mark a specific human group's identity is extremely intriguing. This theory suggests that singing may be related to group identity from the very beginning of human evolution. This brings up some very interesting questions about how and why understanding performance is important to understanding the construction of identity.

Barbara Ehrenreich, who became famous for her bestselling auto-ethnography *Nickel and Dimed* (2001), explores what she calls the 'History of Collective Joy' in her book *Dancing in the Streets: A History of Collective Joy* (2006). Ehrenreich's book is an attempt to explain why, since the beginning of recorded history, and perhaps since prehistoric times, humans have held festivals at which dancing, chanting, and singing is a common element. Ehrenreich imagines a scene from 10,000 years ago:

> You will find humans [...] dancing in lines or circles, sometimes wearing masks or what appear to be costumes, often waving branches or sticks. Most likely, both sexes would be dancing, each in its separate line or circle. Their faces and bodies might be painted with red ochre, or so archaeologists guess from the widespread presence of that colored ore in human settlements.
>
> (Ehrenreich 2006: 21)

Some of the earliest traces of evidence for this behavior can be found in rock art. Rock art are drawings created by prehistoric humans, and is sometimes referred to as 'cave paintings,' because much of the artworks that have been preserved are in caves.

The typical cave where the rock art was found was not inhabited, but appeared to have been some kind of ceremonial site. Rock art has been found at archeological sites in Europe, Africa, Asia, and Australia, dating as early as 100,000 BC, perhaps even earlier. 'Israeli archaeologist Yosef Garfinkel asserts that dancing scenes "were a most popular, indeed almost the only, subject used to describe interaction between people in the Neolithic and Chalcolithic periods"' (Garfinkel qtd. in Ehrenreich 2006: 22). These sort of rituals may go back well into the Paleolithic era, the time before about 10,000 BC when agriculture was introduced to human society.

More evidence for this assertion comes from early anthropological evidence of observations of indigenous societies. These are records from Catholic missionaries, colonists, explorers, anthropologists such as Sir James George Frazer, and scientists such as Baldwin Spencer. Ehrenreich explains that while Europeans were exploring and conquering the 'New World,' they found 'the almost ubiquitous practice of ecstatic ritual, in which the natives would gather to dance, sing, or chant to a state of exhaustion and, beyond that, sometimes trance' (Ehrenreich 2006: 1). Often, the accounts of these colonial encounters employ exoticizing language, and portray the performances that they observed in terms of difference. Take, for example, this quote from Herman Melville as he describes a ritual he saw in Tahiti that he called 'The Lory-Lory':

> Presently, raising a strange chant, they softly sway themselves, gradually quickening the movement, until at length, for a few passionate moments with throbbing bosoms, and glowing cheeks, they abandon themselves to all the spirit of the dance, apparently lost to everything around. But soon subsiding again into the same languid measure as before, the eyes swimming in their heads, join in one wild chorus, and sink into each other's arms.
>
> (Melville qtd. in Moorehead 1966: 30)

In 1963, the anthropologist Erika Bourguignon surveyed the ethnographic literature for instances of ecstatic rituals in indigenous societies, and found that '92 percent of small-scale societies surveyed encouraged some sort of religious trances, in most cases through ecstatic group ritual' (Ehrenreich 2006: 5). It is very probable that in the other 8 per cent of the accounts, the observers may have failed to record rituals that were performed, as this type of behavior was typically seen as unimportant to the European sensibility, or even unfairly interpreted as devil worship or even cannibalism. All of this evidence demonstrates that ritual performances, including dancing, chanting, and (most importantly for this study) singing, have been around perhaps since the dawn of humanity itself, or at least for thousands of years before written language was invented.

Thus, it is very possible that singing may have originated very early in human evolution as a precursor to language, evidenced by the many different kinds of singing and dancing rituals that were observed by early colonists and settlers. There is a long history of public singing, from the ancient Greeks to contemporary Japan, where karaoke was invented. All along the way, one of the recurring themes that echoes back to us from history is the way that singing is a communal act. It is not something that one does (only) in private. History does not record people who sing in the shower. It records those acts of singing that have had significant social and cultural impacts. There seems to be a universal need for humans to sing; and there also seems to be a universal need for humans to sing in groups.

Piano Man

Trey is a good-looking young man in his late twenties with a somewhat muscular build and short, blonde hair. As the KJ calls his name, he grabs a wooden stool from the side of the bar and brings it to the stage. He sits down and reaches into his pocket, bringing out a small harmonica. The song he has chosen to sing is 'Piano Man' by Billy Joel. As the song begins, he plays the harmonica into the microphone. He is very good. This is one of those rare occasions in karaoke, when the audience realizes that the performer is not your average amateur, and the full attention of the bar turns to the singer on stage. Trey begins to sing, and his voice is as trained as his harmonica playing. He sings in a strong, crisp voice, punctuated by his youth, 'It's nine o'clock on a Saturday, the regular crowd shuffles in/There's an old man sitting next to me, making love to his tonic and gin.' The choice of song seems especially good for karaoke at Capone's, telling a story from Joel's early days as a lounge performer, before he was famous. In fact, it was released on his first album, became one of his highest charting singles, and was eventually considered his signature song.

The lyrics pay homage to the other patrons of the bar, who seem to have their own unrealized hopes and broken dreams. There is John, the bartender, who laments, '"Bill, I believe this is killing me," as a smile ran away from his face/"Well, I'm sure that I could be a movie star, if I could get out of this place."' There is Paul, the real-estate agent, 'who never had time for a wife.' There's Davy, who is in the Navy, 'and probably will be for life.' What they all have in common is that they come to the bar to drink and forget their problems, and listen to music. 'They're sharing a drink they call loneliness/But it's better than drinking alone.' The characters in the song also share lives parallel to those of the real-life characters at Capone's. Every one of them has their own story. Each of them has their own hopes and dreams, and they come to sing karaoke here for the warmth of companionship.

By the end of the song, everyone in the bar is singing along with Trey. As he plays the last few notes on his harmonica, the place erupts in a wave of cheers and applause. As quietly as he started, Trey thanks the crowd and moves the stool back to the bar. Later on that evening, I have a chance to talk to him and compliment him on his performance. I mention his harmonica playing and singing ability. He tells me that he is a professional musician, which does not surprise me. What does surprise me is that he is the lead singer of a local thrash metal band. I ask him why he would choose to sing a Billy Joel song, so different from the music that he usually sings. He tells me, 'It's nice to do something different for a change.'

Trey's performance was one of the best I ever witnessed during my study. For the hundreds of bad singers that I suffered through, I got to hear a few exceptionally good singers. It made me wonder why Trey, who is an accomplished musician on his own, would come and sing at Capone's. Eventually, I concluded that it must be connected to the sense of community that one feels a part of when singing in front of a crowd. This led me to a very important realization. Perhaps, our culture's obsession with celebrity is actually a longing for community. When we dream of being a star, of being on a stage with thousands of fans adoring us, what we are really dreaming about is being at the center of a human connection that, in this alienating postmodern age of technology, is missing from our lives.

The History of Public Singing

Some of the first evidence related to public singing in recorded history is the same evidence that has been used to speculate about the origins of theater. Ehrenreich explains, 'It was the Greeks [...] who left us the clearest evidence of ecstatic ritual behavior. [...] Dance [...] was a central and defining activity of the ancient Greek community: line and circle dances, dances of young men or young women or both together, dances at regularly scheduled festivities, [...] dances for victory, for the gods, or for the sheer fun of it' (Ehrenreich 2006: 32). As an example of how these ancient rituals might have looked, Ehrenreich suggests that these rituals might have been similar to the maenadism depicted in Euripides' play *The Bacchae*. It is often supposed that Greek drama is a direct descendant of the dithyrambic choruses that were presented in ancient Greece to honor Dionysus.

One of the best overviews of historical singing traditions in European culture appears in the book *Karaoke: The Global Phenomenon* (2007), by Zhou Xun and Francesca Tarocco. Interestingly enough, many of the singing traditions in Europe originated in pagan rituals that were eventually appropriated by the Catholic Church. They write, 'Centuries ago people in Europe began to celebrate the winter solstice with public singing and dancing. Most [...] songs were joyful in tone, intended to raise the spirits. Early Christians took on this essentially pagan practice from around AD 129 and introduced the "Angel's Hymn" ("Gloria in excelsis")' (Xun and Tarocco 2007: 23). Singing played a large part in the Catholic Mass, and it still does today. In fact, the reintroduction of official (recorded) theater to Europe at the end of the Dark Ages was around AD 925, when 'tropes' were added to the Church service. A trope is an extended musical passage sung by a choir. The first known recorded performance of this kind was performed for an Easter service, and was titled *Quem Quaeritis* ('Whom do you seek?'). In the performance of this trope, the two sides of a choir would sing the story of the resurrection. The performance of this trope eventually became theatrical, with the addition of actors to add action, and the altar serving as the tomb.

Another example of amateur singing is the Christmas carol. By 1223, Saint Francis of Assisi introduced the nativity play in Italy, and the practice of performing nativity plays and singing Christmas carols soon spread across the rest of Europe. In addition to singing in the Catholic Church, singing became integral to many Protestant Church services as well, with many hymns being written for particular denominations. Singing Christmas carols was very popular in England during the Elizabethan period. During the Renaissance, most Christmas carolers were traveling minstrels. Although the lyrics of these songs usually told the Christmas story, these performances were primarily for entertainment, and not religious.

After the Puritan Revolution, theater and music were banned in England, but public singing became even more popular after the restoration of the monarchy. During the eighteenth and nineteenth centuries, chanson singers and mummers continued the tradition of the minstrels, traveling across both western and eastern Europe, traveling door-to-door to bring songs to their neighbors.

In the nineteenth century in England, pubs, beer halls, and gin palaces became places for public singing with the establishment of choral societies. At first this location was out of convenience, because the pub was a central location, and made it easy for these clubs to meet. Eventually, singing in pubs, beer halls, and gin palaces gave way to the beginning of the music hall tradition. In the more respectable parts of town, music halls were first built to cater to upper-class audiences, as an alternative to the pubs. Xun and Tarocco describe the music hall scene, 'A typical music hall song consists of a series of verses, sung by the performer alone, and a repeated chorus carrying the principal melody, and the audience is encouraged to join in' (Xun and Tarocco 2007: 24). Music halls would later give rise to Vaudeville in America, and the rise of musical theater. The connection between public singing and drinking establishments was a significant step toward the eventual invention of karaoke.

Mr. Brightside

It is my birthday. I am turning the grand old age of thirty-nine. I will realize later, looking back, that any age in one's thirties is actually very young. However, tonight I feel old. It has been almost a year since my divorce was finalized. I recently started a Facebook account. To celebrate, I have decided to organize a karaoke outing at a local bar in Boulder (not Capone's) using Facebook's 'event' function. Many people fear that the rise of the computer age and the intrusion of Internet technologies into our lives are a bad thing, destined to take away our humanity and dissolve our communities.

In 2000, political scientist Robert D. Putnam published the book *Bowling Alone: The Collapse and Revival of American Community*. Putnam writes about how, during the second half of the twentieth century, there was an overall decline of 'social capital,' benefits to society that resulted from the collective membership of individuals in groups. He traces several aspects of this decline, including an overall trend of moving the control mechanism of social groups from the local to the national level. Some of the examples he gives are various political, civic, church-based, and work-related groups, such as the American Association of Retired Persons, Elks Clubs, Kiwanis, Rotary, National Association for the Advancement of Colored People, Boy Scouts, and Alcoholics Anonymous, just to name a few. Although membership in many of these groups is up on a national level, participation at the local level has fallen. Putnam uses the metaphor of bowling. Although more people bowl every year, people are less likely to join a local bowling league today than they were decades ago. Thus, people no longer bowl in groups, but are 'bowling alone.'

Putnam attributes much of this trend to the rise of technology, such as computers and the Internet.

People often have similar reactions to karaoke technology, seeing it as yet another trapping of the digital age, as 'commodified' and 'canned,' a danger to 'real' artistic expression. They see karaoke as something that is taking away our humanity and our ability to socialize. I tend to think that, although there are certainly dangers of technology taking over our lives as people become addicted to their screens in lieu of living, present interactions with fellow human beings, there is a bright side to computer technology and social networks as well. Human beings are social creatures, and we will always find new ways to be social and build community. Seen in this light, the constant reinvention and application of technology to social processes is just another example of how human beings constantly find new ways to connect with one another. My idea to organize a karaoke birthday party over Facebook is an example of one of the positive ways that these new digital technologies can be employed.

For one thing, I recently reconnected with several good friends of mine that I had lost track of over the years. One is a former suite-mate from college. Another, oddly enough, is an ex-girlfriend, who I have not seen in over fifteen years, and brings her husband along in tow. Another fellow karaoke traveler who makes it to my birthday celebration is Lauren, a young woman who I recently met at a Christmas party held at the house of one of my mother's friends. We had talked during dinner and found that we had much in common. After dinner, we continued our pleasant conversation, and before I left the party, I asked her if she was on Facebook, and we connected and began corresponding online. These days, when I meet new people, I am more often asked to 'friend' them on Facebook than asked to exchange phone numbers or e-mail addresses. Within the next week, I asked Lauren if she would like to go out with me and sing karaoke. Lucky for me, she said 'yes,' further demonstrating the 'ice-breaking' function that karaoke sometimes serves in social contexts. Although this example may seem, at first, like a departure from traditional forms of courtship, it is yet another example of how new technologies are being used to make human connections rather than sever them.

It is great to reconnect with these people who I have not seen in many years, friends who meant so much to me earlier in my life. It is also great to connect with new people in my life and get to know them better. It is a wonderful night. Singing with my friends makes me forget that I am one year older. I realize that my many nights spent in a karaoke bar, talking to random people and performing in front of them on stage, has made me more confident and socially adept. I do not realize it at this time, but Lauren and I will soon begin dating, and eventually she will become my wife. I tell this story because it is a great example of the way that karaoke, and perhaps other forms of social technology, can have a positive impact on our lives and help us to connect with our friends, as well as build and maintain communities. Thus, although people in contemporary society may be more likely to bowl alone, they are more and more likely, at least here in the beginning of the twenty-first century, to sing in groups.

Performing Community

Ultimately, the meaning of individual identity is not significant unless it is constructed within the context of a community. A common metaphor used to describe a person's agency is the 'voice.' Yet, the idea that the voice is one's agency goes beyond the realm of literary metaphor. In some sense, the voice is literally one's agency. The power of one individual in this world is largely insignificant, but agency is enacted when one's individual desires are transferred to and enacted upon by the community. This is true of both literal and metaphorical voices as well. Let us say, for example, a person is born without vocal cords. Would this disability mean that they have lost their agency because they have lost their voice? Of course not. However, that person would have to find ways other than the voice to enact their agency within their community. They might learn Sign Language, or use a computer or some other kind of technology to assist them in communicating their desires. Yet, the fact remains that these are all kinds of performances. In fact, one can say that it is performance itself that constitutes agency.

One of the most interesting articles I have ever read about karaoke is by the musicologist Dan Cusic, called 'Karaoke: High Tech and the Folk Tradition,' published in the Tennessee Folklore Society Bulletin. Cusic proposes that karaoke is the modern-day version of folk singing. He writes about an essay by G. K. Chesterton called 'The Little Birds Who Won't Sing': 'G. K. Chesterton bemoans the fact that people no longer sing when they work. He notes that, in the past, "there were songs for reapers reaping and songs for sailors hauling ropes." [...] Chesterton asks, "If reapers sing while reaping, why should not auditors sing while auditing and bankers while banking?"'(Chesterton qtd. in Cusic 1991: 52).

Cusic attempts to answer this question by suggesting that one reason for the disappearance of the folk song is the general migration of the population from rural to urban localities. This cultural transformation, which began with the industrial revolution, has resulted in a litany of cultural changes that have affected the way contemporary people view performance. Some of the changes that Cusic writes about include the crowded nature of urban environments, the intrusion of televisions and radios playing in public spaces, the way that record companies have conditioned us to be passive rather than active consumers of music, and the loss of oral traditions that serve as examples of the way that people can sing with each other. Cusic laments, 'We have lost the oral tradition and have no family models to teach us songs, sing with us, or show us the role that singing should play in our lives' (Cusic 1991: 52).

Is karaoke, then, even more evidence that folk singing is on its way out? Are karaoke machines insidiously replacing live folk musicians? Cusic suggests that, actually, the opposite is true. Karaoke is keeping folk singing alive. He writes, 'But folk singing is not a thing of the past because, if you listen, you can still hear a lot of folks singing. They sing in their cars, walking along sidewalks, in the shower, in the roaring traffic's boom, or the silence of a lonely room' (Cusic 1991: 53). According to Cusic, karaoke is a very good example of this kind of modern-day folk singing. Karaoke qualifies as folk singing for several reasons. First, folk singing is often defined as songs known by a majority of people in a given culture that are passed from person to person. Cusic argues that this same behavior can be observed when people sing karaoke, and the audience knows the songs as well. 'The fact is that people know the words and melody, they've learned them from hearing them sung before – by the "original" artist or singer who first made the song nationally famous in most cases – and thus this is folk singing and proof that the folk tradition in song is alive and well in today's technological culture' (Cusic 1991: 54). Karaoke is the logical, modern-day manifestation of folk singing, the tendency of people to sing in communities. Thus, singing karaoke is often seen to have a connection to a sense of collective identity, a 'voice' that defines a community.

From my own experiences, some of the most memorable and rewarding karaoke performances I ever had were times when the entire crowd was singing along with me. Even in the years after my karaoke study was over, on those rare occasions when I would go out and sing again, I would try to gauge the demographics of the audience and choose a song that would encourage group singing. Some recent success stories include getting a bar full of college students to sing along with me to Weezer's 'Say it Ain't So,' one of my favorite go-to songs. Then, a couple of weeks later, when visiting a rural bar in the middle of Missouri wine country, having a bar full of strangers join me for a rendition of 'Free Bird' by Lynyrd Skynyrd. The sing-along is the ultimate karaoke high. It may be the primary reason why Neil Diamond still collects residual royalties for his song 'Sweet Caroline.' The sing-along is the closest you can get to karaoke celebrity. It guarantees an amazing adrenaline rush, because it is the embodiment of the metaphorical merging of the self with the community. I suggest you try it some time.

This is not to say that everything is always roses and rainbows when it comes to the manifestation of community within karaoke performances. The flip-side of the positive aspects of the formation of karaoke community is the phenomenon of the 'regulars' versus the 'tourists.' In karaoke vocabulary, regulars are patrons who come to the same karaoke bar week after week, and come to be known by the KJ, the bar staff, singers, and other bar patrons. 'Tourists,' on the other hand, are people who come to a karaoke bar for one night and never come back again.

I have heard stories from people who have gone out to sing karaoke and have been treated rudely by the people that they have encountered. I have personally experienced this treatment myself. Typically, this treatment manifests in the form of not getting called up right away to sing, or watching 'regular' patrons called up to sing multiple times before getting to sing at all. I am not entirely certain what causes this phenomenon, but I expect that it may occur because many of the 'tourists' who show up at bars to sing do not take their singing seriously, get extremely drunk, and make a joke out of their performance. Thus, regular singers at karaoke bars may be skeptical of a new singer that they have never seen at the bar before.

Although, on the surface, the existence of this phenomenon might seem to undermine my argument that karaoke singing helps to construct community, I would argue that it actually reinforces my argument. Part of community formation, especially when viewed on an evolutionary level, is about determining who is in the 'in-group' and who is in the 'out-group.' In the case of the 'tourists' versus the 'regulars,' regular karaoke community members are behaving in a way that is positive and reinforcing toward the members that they consider part of the 'in-group,' and is negative and disciplinary to the tourists, who they consider part of the 'out-group.'

Local Celebrity

Toward the end of my ethnographic study, I had my own personal experience of celebrity. My career in karaoke started without a fanfare. During my first several months of singing, I was not very good. Occasionally, I had a breakout performance in which I surprised both the audience and myself. I had a particularly humbling experience early on in my study when I chose to sing the song 'Stairway to Heaven,' by Led Zeppelin. I chose this song because I consider it one of the great anthems of rock, and also because I have heard it so many times that I was convinced I knew the words and the tune. I had forgotten, however, about the end of the song, when Robert Plant begins to sing in an inhumanly high range. I also forgot that there is a several-minute guitar solo in the middle of the song, during which I was forced to stand awkwardly on stage as the music continued to play on and on. This was my first lesson: one of the most important factors in karaoke success is the choice of the song.

On the other hand, there was the first time I ever sang the Moody Blues song 'Nights in White Satin.' As the end of the song neared, I suddenly remembered the very high notes when the lead singer repeatedly sings, 'I love you/Yes I love you/Oh how I love you.' Each of these lines is sung with a higher and higher vocalization. Although I was scared that I could not sing that high, I surprised myself. As the end of the song neared, I found myself using my falsetto voice to reach each higher and higher pitch. I remembered a microphone technique that my stepfather, who used to sing weekly in the Church choir, had told me about. I held the microphone closer to my mouth and sang with less air (thus less volume), and I was able to produce higher and higher notes. When I finished the song, a loud wave of applause greeted me, and I basked in the glow of accomplishment.

After this occasion, there were numerous other times when I began to break out of my musical shell, and I began to get better and better at singing. One day, when I was bragging to a friend about my newfound karaoke prowess, he asked me how I knew I was good and suggested that maybe I was just imagining that I was good. I paused, and then replied, 'I can tell because of the audience.' It was true, although to some degree I could tell I was becoming better because I could hear myself getting better, the only way that I could really tell was by the reaction of the audience. Each week it seemed like the applause I received was getting louder and louder. Drew explains this phenomenon, 'Karaoke stardom translates as a kind of local celebrity. Indeed, a certain buzz often follows the most charismatic singers on the local karaoke circuit whose performances might be greeted with a flourish of cigarette lighters or a hail of apartment keys' (Drew 2001: 14).

Pretty soon, I began to get requests to sing certain songs from the audience. Nancy, the bartender, would occasionally encourage me to sing songs by the Rolling Stones, and Anna, the lead waitress, would encourage me to do songs by The Who. One of my friends, a young girl named Barbara, would turn in karaoke slips to the KJ with my name on them without me knowing. I would find myself being called up to the stage to sing the Journey song 'Open Arms,' even though I was not the one to turn in the request slip or choose the song. One day I was running errands in town, getting the power steering on my Pontiac Grand Am fixed at the local Midas shop. After I paid for the repairs and I was walking out to the parking lot, one of the mechanics, a large, gray-bearded, middle-aged Latino man, began waving at me. At first, I thought that he looked familiar, but I was unsure where I had met him. I tentatively waved back at him, and got in my car and drove away. As I was leaving the parking lot I realized that, although I had never spoken to him in person, he was a frequent customer at Capone's. I had often seen him playing pool with a group of Latino men in one of the back rooms while I sang karaoke. I had just encountered my first fan. I had become a local celebrity.

This event also gave me a greater appreciation of the power of karaoke that, as a social force, can unite very diverse members of a community. Here was a man who I never had spoken to, and perhaps would never have spoken to in the everyday course of my life, someone who may not even speak the same language that I do, and I had made a connection to him through the magic of karaoke. I remember the first time that I sang the song 'Smells Like Teen Spirit' by Nirvana. As I approached the chorus, I realized that several people in the audience were beginning to sing along with me, 'With the lights out it's less dangerous. Here we are now, entertain us/I feel stupid and contagious/Here we are now, entertain us.' I often think about this song as the anthem of Generation X, with its detached, self-deprecating irony. That night, the song crossed generational barriers. Many of the people in the audience who were singing along with me were either much younger than me or much older than me. Although most of the background singers were men, some of the women joined along as well. Eventually, I began to realize that people singing along with you was the ultimate compliment. Paradoxically, the quintessential moment of stardom comes when the community merges their performance with the performance of the artist. Thus, I realized that the performance of the community is much more powerful than the performance of the individual. Individual agency can only be achieved from the blessings of the masses.

Finale

At the beginning of this book, I told a story about an incident I observed at Capone's, an altercation between a young Latino man named Kenny and a young country music singer named Jennifer. To summarize, Kenny and some of his friends arrived at Capone's late at night, and Kenny began to create quite a ruckus, mainly through his performance of karaoke. Among other epithets thrown during that performance, the first words out of Kenny's mouth into the microphone were 'less fuckin' country,' and then he broke into the alternative rock song 'Poison,' by Bell Biv Devoe. Later, when Jennifer was singing the country song 'Crazy,' Kenny repeatedly interrupted Jennifer's singing to tell her that she was singing the song incorrectly. She did not take this well, gave Kenny the finger, and threatened him with violence by her boyfriend, 'He's gonna kick your ass if you don't shut up!' Luckily no actual violence broke out that night. Seemingly, whatever cultural tensions led to this altercation were also diffused through the performance of karaoke.

When I told this story in the introduction, I invited the reader to answer this question, did the conflict in this example arise because of tensions due to: (A) gender, (B) ethnicity, (C) class, or (D) all of the above. I invite you to consider the way you used to understand the performance of identity, and how that understanding may have shifted during the experience of reading this book. Do you feel like you understand more or less than when you started this process? I suspect that you have found that you now have a lot more to think about than when you first encountered this example.

When I first witnessed this performance, and attempted to unravel the cultural underpinnings of the situation, my initial instinct was to attribute the conflict to the performance of ethnicity. Surely, the fact that Kenny was Latino and Jennifer was Caucasian was the most visually apparent source of the conflict. Ethnicity is often pointed to as the cause of political infighting between cultural groups. Ethnic conflicts have been going on since the beginning of recorded history, so that seemed like a plausible explanation.

But then, I started thinking about the fact that Jennifer involved her boyfriend in the verbal scuffle, and also the fact that Kenny acted effeminately, drawing attention to himself at a site where the normative sexuality is straight. So, I began to think that maybe the cultural tension arose from the performance of gender. Perhaps Kenny's attack on country music was a way for him to attempt to reclaim power that he felt had been taken from him as a member of a subjugated gender group. Even if Kenny is not gay, which is impossible to tell based on observation alone, the perception that his performance did not fall in line with heteronormative expectations might be enough to create friction. Or, perhaps Jennifer's invocation of her boyfriend was her way of defending herself against Kenny's verbal attacks. She was performing her relationship in order to demonstrate her power over him.

But that does not completely explain this event either. One of the more subtle things that I observed in this altercation was that Jennifer seemed to be dressed very modestly in simple clothing, while Kenny's clothes were very flashy. This led me to hypothesize that Kenny might be wealthier than Jennifer is, and thus come from a higher economic class. If this is true, then class difference was also being played out. One sign that this could be the case is the way that Kenny's tirade began as a general attack on country music, and only later did he single out Jennifer as a symbolic member of a group of people who sing country music. The other element that is key to understanding this is the context of the bar itself. One of the most popular kinds of music sung at Capone's karaoke night is country music, and the most common clientele at Capone's are lower- to lower-middle class. Understood against this background, the entire event could be attributed to class conflict.

Eventually, I concluded that all of these factors came into play. In fact, what made the incident so explosive was the confluence of differences within the various performances of gender, ethnicity, and class that were happening simultaneously in the same cultural space. On the other hand, the fact that these differences were exposed and diffused within the context of a performance, and not as actual acts of violence, is notable as well. This event serves as an example of several factors related to the performance of identity. First, it shows that people often perform aspects of their identity in public as a way to demonstrate their allegiances with various cultural groups. Furthermore, the allegiances that these performative identifications imply are constantly in flux. Eventually, performances of identity (and thus identification with a particular cultural group) lead to the assimilation of individuals into communities. Finally, the function of the performance of identity is to serve as a point of catharsis, to ensure that cultural conflicts that could escalate into violent confrontations are resolved within a more peaceful context. So, although there may be more than one correct answer to the question I posed, I argue that the correct response to the question is (D) all of the above.

For myself, I have to say that I understand the performance of gender, ethnicity, and class to a much greater degree than when I started this journey. At the same time, the knowledge that I have acquired in this study, and have attempted to communicate to you through this writing, has perhaps led to more questions than it has answered. But the paradigm shift is undeniable. During the first stages of planning my study, I began by asking the question of whether or not people who sing karaoke perform their identities. The answer is 'yes and no.' Once I began to observe karaoke singers, I slowly became convinced that people perform gender, ethnicity, and class. Yet, I was also surprised by the ways that people performed identities that were not their own. This established my conviction that karaoke performance is a sort of free-floating field of play, in which people can perform their own identities, but, if they want to, they can also try on other identities for size.

In this way, in addition to helping to demonstrate the ways that human identity is constructed through small performances that occur all around us in everyday life, karaoke provides a space of cultural production where performances of identity are not only constructed, but also subverted. A person's identity is defined by a performed boundary, enacted between the way that they define themselves and the way that society defines them. Thus, although karaoke singing begins with the desire of an individual performer, it ends with the acceptance of the audience. The performance of cultural categories such as gender, ethnicity, and class defines the relationship between the individual and the community.

Coda

A friend of mine asked me recently if I was going to keep singing karaoke even after my study was over. At first I did not know the answer to this question. I guess that I had naturally assumed that I would gradually phase out my karaoke singing and eventually stop altogether. The thing is, the more that I think about it, the more I feel I will keep singing. I began my study with a desire to find out why other people perform their identities. Eventually, I realized that I learned more about myself and my own sense of identity than I could ever learn from observing other people. Because I threw myself into my research and decided to not only observe karaoke, but also sing it, the experience has so profoundly affected my life that it has become a part of who I am. Because of my karaoke singing, I have gained self-confidence. I am happier now. I have a better grip of who I am. I have learned a new way to express my creativity. Singing karaoke helped me to find my voice.

Beyond this, one of the most unexpected results of my research has been the friends that I made while singing karaoke. When I first started my study, I would sit by myself at my table. Eventually, I got up the nerve to introduce myself to new people. Although I have always been a very shy person, I found that if you go up to a group of people sitting at a table, and ask them if they mind if you sit with them, they are happy to share their friendship with you. My advice to you, if you consider yourself a wallflower, if you have a hard time making friends: go to a karaoke night and introduce yourself to the nice people who are there. Not everyone has a place that they can go where 'everybody knows your name.' It will be hard to give all of this up. I would have never expected that when I started all of this, that I would end up finding my community.

Encore

It has been several years now since I completed my karaoke study. Shortly after I defended my dissertation and received my Ph.D. in theater, I received a job offer at a small university in Missouri. So, I upended the life that I had built for myself in Colorado, packed up my belongings, and set off for the Midwest. I was lucky enough to talk Lauren, who was then my girlfriend, into moving along with me, bringing the three dogs that we owned between us. After a year of working at Missouri Western State University in St. Joseph, Missouri,

I received a job offer at the University of Missouri, a large research school in Columbia, Missouri. Last year, Lauren and I were married. This happy event brought me full circle. I had overcome the messy divorce and discontentment that I had been feeling with my life at the beginning of this story, and was starting a happy new life with a wonderful woman.

I am very busy now, teaching, writing, and directing a play each year. I do not have as much time for karaoke as I used to, but every once in a while I manage to go out to a small karaoke bar here in downtown Columbia. I have made it a tradition to take the cast of each of the plays I direct to sing karaoke on closing night of each of my plays. The cast and I usually sing the Queen song 'Bohemian Rhapsody' in unison as the last song of the night. Every once in a while, I find myself downtown on karaoke night, and I will pop in to sing a few songs. I have to say, though, that it is just not the same. What I miss the most is the community of people that I got to know during my study. Since I do not go to karaoke as regularly as I used to, I have not been able to make the kind of karaoke friends that I used to know. I am sure that eventually I will meet new friends and build new connections, but I will never forget my friends at Capone's.

Afterword

Karaoke as Performance Reactivation

by Philip Auslander

One of the issues I have addressed in my work over the past decade is the vexed question of performance art documentation (see Auslander 2006, 2009, 2014). My intention has been to challenge a critical discourse that seems to be almost entirely preoccupied with the ontological relationship between the 'original' performance and the documents (e.g., photographs, video recordings, or written descriptions) that presume to capture it and make it available to audiences beyond those who experienced the live event. I wish to shift the focus of this conversation from the relationship between the performance and its documentation, which is frequently characterized as inevitably a relationship of inadequacy and betrayal, to the audience that is in the position of experiencing the performance from its documentation (see Auslander 2006). I am interested in arriving at a theoretical account of how this audience retrieves the performance from its documentation. Kevin Brown's richly informative and engaging investigation of karaoke performance as a social and cultural practice has led me to think about how karaoke fits into my theoretical narrative.

In trying to think through these issues, I have taken great inspiration from a passage in Walter Benjamin's 'The Work of Art in the Age of Mechanical Reproduction':

> [t]echnical reproduction can put the copy of the original into situations which would be out of reach for the original itself. Above all, it enables the original to meet the beholder halfway, be it in the form of a photograph or phonograph record. The cathedral leaves its locale to be received in the studio of a lover of art; the choral production, performed in an auditorium or in the open air, resounds in the living room ... [I]n permitting the reproduction to meet the beholder or listener in his own particular situation, [the technique of reproduction] reactivates the object reproduced.
>
> (1969: 222)

I find the idea of *reactivation* that Benjamin introduces at the end of this passage to be a thought-provoking description of the process on which I am trying to get a grip. In Benjamin's account, the reproduction (document) of an art object or performance does not simply enable a second-hand experience of the thing reproduced. Rather, it somehow allows us to re-produce the thing reproduced for ourselves, to bring it to life, to reactivate it, so as to be able to experience it in our present moment. Listening to recorded music is perhaps the most straightforward example: we hear the music unfurling for us in our 'particular situation' even though it was recorded at some other time in some other place, and the recording, the document, is what makes this possible. I take the process by which we experience a work of performance art through its documentation to be similar.

I have provided a detailed phenomenological analysis of what this process may entail elsewhere (see Auslander 2009). Here, I want to emphasize that reactivation, as I understand it, is something the audience for a reproduced artwork or performance *does* – it is not something that simply happens when we behold a reproduction. Through an act of consciousness, we establish a relationship with the reproduced performance that allows us to perceive it as immediate. However, the idea that reactivation is something that happens primarily in the mind no longer strikes me as completely adequate. It seems to me quite clear that there are also modes of corporeal engagement with reproduced performances that respond to the 'participative longings' performances evoke and constitute another kind of reactivation (Appleyard 1991).

Reactivation, as described by Benjamin, posits the beholder of the reproduction as a spectator (albeit, in my formulation, not a passive one) experiencing a work of art or artistic performance. I suggest that reactivation is also an act that can constitute us as *performers* across a cultural spectrum far broader than the field of art. I'm thinking of a range of activities that includes air guitar; the extraordinary variety of things people re-enact for the purpose of posting videos on Internet hosting sites such as YouTube; some kinds of video game play, including music-themed games such as *Guitar Hero* and *Rock Band*; and, yes, karaoke. All of these activities, and many others like them, reflect the impulse not just to experience the reactivated performance mentally from a spectatorial position, but also to experience it from the performer's embodied perspective, to gain some sense of *how it feels to do it*. In her ethnographic account of gamers who play musical video games, Kiri Miller describes what I take to be the essence of corporeal reactivation: '*Guitar Hero* and *Rock Band* let players put the performance back into recorded music, reanimating it with their physical engagement and adrenaline' (2012: 49). In terms of performance art, this impulse has led to a spate of re-enactments of historical works, described by Mechtild Widrich as 're-performance, the restaging of performances by an artist decades after the fact, be it the original artist, a contemporary, or the representative of a younger generation, eager to "live through their heritage"' (2014: 140).

Karaoke is significantly different from this latter kind of re-performance, of course. For one thing, karaoke singers are not artists in their own right in the same category as those who originally recorded the songs they sing. Karaoke thus is not a matter of artists reproducing other artists' work but, rather, of amateur enactments of songs often associated with well-known, professional artists. In performance art, the question of just how accurate a re-performance can or should be is an open one, but the concept does entail some notion of fidelity to an earlier event. By contrast, karaoke performers do not necessarily attempt to recreate specific events, though they may. The mimetic dimension of karaoke varies with its cultural context. Whereas Japanese performers are often reluctant to depart from replicating canonical recorded versions of songs, singers in the US, UK, and Sweden are more interested in stamping the karaoke repertoire with their individuality (see Mitsui and

Hosokawa 1998, Drew 2004, Kelly 1998, and Fornäs 1998). It is well known that on *American Idol*, the US television singing competition, judges regularly use the word karaoke as a term of opprobrium that means the singer failed to 'make the song [his or her] own.' William H. Kelly, discussing the British karaoke scene, describes the singers' use of existing songs as:

> the appropriation of popular songs from the exclusive realm of the professional singer by karaoke amateurs who make them their own, thus closing the gap between amateur and professional. This represents a shift from a close identification between professional singer and song to a disproportionate emphasis on the song itself which has been reinvented for the karaoke format and the amateur singer.
>
> (1998: 87)

Understood in this way, karaoke performance brings into being a new performance of what is, in effect, a new piece of music rather than a recreation of an existing performance.

Sometimes, this process of appropriating a song leads to a kind of karaoke celebrity. Singers in this category are called upon to repeat their performances in ways that parallel conventional performance norms:

> Others will attend just to hear them sing, and they'll receive requests to do particular songs . . . (in the men's room at the bar Hector attended, the graffiti read, 'Hector Rules, Ask For Him To Sing'). Often these performers have signature tunes that they are almost obligated to perform. At yet another bar the emcee tells me, 'Joe and Jack couldn't come to Spender's without doing "Sweet Emotion"—the crowd would kill them.'
>
> (Drew 2004: 72)

In this way, the new, karaoke performance of the song supplants existing recordings as the object of repetition.

Although these accounts suggest that karaoke, at least in the West, is generally more about treating the songs as raw material for self-expressive performances than about impersonating the artists with whom the songs are associated or recreating particular performances (unlike a tribute band such as the Dark Star Orchestra that recreates specific performances by the Grateful Dead), karaoke performances are inevitably intertextual with the recordings of the songs that made them popular or famous enough to become fodder for karaoke singers. Rebecca Schneider describes re-performance practices that include both restaged performance art works and Civil War re-enactments as 'the replay of evidence (photographs, documents, archival remains) back across the body in gestic negotiation' (2011: 9). This description applies equally well to karaoke performances, in which one kind of evidence (the words of the song) is literally replayed as the lyrics scroll down the screen, and the archive is invoked, perhaps distantly, through the unavoidable referencing of earlier performances of the same material. The singer's performance constitutes the 'gestic negotiation' with the bodies of evidence Schneider posits.

That said, however much karaoke may implicitly refer to the past histories of the songs, the emphasis in karaoke performance is decidedly on the present moment. Schneider problematizes the idea of the immediacy of the present by asking (and glossing Richard Schechner and Judith Butler in so doing), 'Does [the present] not take place or become composed in double, triple, or multiple time – especially if performance and the "sedimented acts" that comprise the social are already a matter of "twice-behaved behavior"?' (2011: 92) Fair enough. As I have suggested, however much karaoke performances supplant existing recorded performances, they cannot be free of references to the past embedded in the songs and their performance histories. We can, however, accept that all performance is temporally complex in the way Schneider suggests while also insisting that different genres of performance navigate this complexity in different ways.

Whereas Civil War re-enactment is 'a clear-cut case of the effort to play one time in another time' (Schneider 2011: 10) and re-performances of performance art works may reflect the desire for 'an authentic return to an event independent of time' (Widrich 2014: 142), karaoke suppresses the song's history and the history of its previous performances and valorizes the moment in the club or bar when someone, often in spite of stage fright or social reservations, stands up to sing, even if the present cannot be treated as a simple or unproblematic concept. Whereas Civil War re-enactors measure the authenticity of their stagings in terms of their fidelity to the past as they understand it, and the authenticity of performance art re-performance is often measured by the degree to which the piece is shown to be 'independent of time' (that is, still aesthetically significant) the authenticity of karaoke performance is measured by the energy, enthusiasm, originality, and commitment of the performers, largely independent of their skill (though a measure of skill is preferred) and with no explicit reference to the song as a specifically historical object that may be performed correctly or incorrectly.

The documentary film *Marina Abramovic: The Artist is Present* (Aker 2012) chronicles Abramovic's retrospective at the Museum of Modern Art in 2010 and the epic durational performance she undertook there for which she sat in the museum's atrium each day of the exhibition for the entire time the museum was open and invited members of the public to sit opposite her. The performance became something of a media event, and people lined up to sit opposite the artist for a few minutes as if it had been a big-ticket rock show. One man had the number of times he participated in the piece (21) tattooed on his arm, while others lined up for hours or camped out overnight in front of the museum in hope of getting a chance to participate. Late in the film, there is a scene of the spectators who have made it into the museum and are watching others experience their time with Abramovic. In this crowd, we see two pairs of people, each consisting of a male and a female. One pair is of young children, perhaps ten years old, while the other is a couple of young adults. In both cases, they are sitting or lying opposite one another and looking intently into one another's eyes. In other words, rather than simply await their turns with Abramovic, they are performing her piece for themselves.

This is karaoke performance art. I mean by this that it is a type of re-performance that is different from those discussed by Schneider (2011) or Widrich (2014) in a number of important ways. First is its amateur status, derived from the fact that the performers are not themselves performance artists responding to the history of their field, but simply people responding to the impulse to find out what it feels like to perform this piece. Second is the fact that because these re-enactments are simultaneous with the performance they recreate (in this admittedly peculiar case) they do not count as historical re-performances. Rather, Abramovic's piece functions more in the way a song does in karaoke, as primarily a pretext for a fresh performance in the present rather than an historical artifact. As with karaoke, the spectators' performances of *The Artist Is Present* are re-activations, rather than re-performances, by means of which spectators-as-performers bring the performance into their 'particular situation' by embodying it. If thinking about karaoke in relation to other practices of re-performance, re-enactment, and re-activation sheds some light on the temporality of karaoke performance and its relationship to previous performances of the same music, it also shows that these practices are distributed across a wide cultural field that extends far beyond the reaches of the art world or the simulated Civil War battlefield.

References

Akers, M. (2012), *Marina Abramovic: The Artist is Present*, Los Angeles: Show of Force.

Appleyard, B. (1991), 'Karaoke Comes to the City of London', *The Sunday Times*, 8 December, http://bryanappleyard.com/karaoke/, Accessed 18 February 2015.

Auslander, P. (2006), 'The Performativity of Performance Documentation', *Performing Arts Journal*, 84, pp. 1–10.

Auslander, P. (2009), 'Reactivation: Performance, Mediatization, and the Present Moment', in M. Chatzichristodoulou, J. Jefferies, and R. Zerihan (eds.), *Interfaces of Performance*, Farnham: Ashgate, pp. 81–93.

Auslander, P. (2014), 'Surrogate Performances: Performance Documentation and the New York Avant-Garde, ca. 1964–74', in E. Carpenter (ed.), *On Performativity*, Vol. 1 of *Living Collections Catalogue*. Minneapolis: Walker Art Center, http://walkerart.org/collections/publications/performativity/surrogate-performances, Accessed 18 February 2015.

Benjamin, W. (1969), 'The Work of Art in the Age of Mechanical Reproduction', H. Zone (trans.) in H. Arendt (ed.), *Illuminations*, New York: Schocken, pp. 217–251.

Drew, R. (2004), '"Scenes" Dimensions of Karaoke in the United States', in A. Bennett and R. A. Peterson (eds.), *Music Scenes: Local, Translocal, and Virtual,* Nashville: Vanderbilt University Press, pp. 64–79.

Fornäs, J. (1998), 'Filling voids along the byway: Identification and interpretation in the Swedish forms of karaoke', in T. Mitsui and S. Hosokawa (eds.), *Karaoke Around the World: Global Technology, Local Singing*, London and New York: Routledge, pp. 115–131.

Kelly, W. H. (1998), 'The adaptability of karaoke in the United Kingdom', in T. Mitsui and S. Hosokawa (eds.), *Karaoke Around the World: Global Technology, Local Singing*, London and New York: Routledge, pp. 81–98.

Miller, K. (2012), *Playing Along: Digital Games, YouTube, and Virtual Performance*, New York: Oxford University Press.

Mitsui, T. and Hosokawa, S. (1998), 'Introduction', in T. Mitsui and S. Hosokawa (eds.), *Karaoke Around the World: Global Technology, Local Singing*, London and New York: Routledge, pp. 1–26.

Schneider, R. (2011), *Performing Remains: Art and War in Times of Theatrical Reenactment*, London and New York: Routledge.

Widrich, M. (2014), 'Is the "Re" in Re-enactment the Same as the "Re" in Re-performance?', in C. Dertnig and F. Thun-Hohenstein (eds.), *Performing the Sentence: Research and Teaching in the Performative Fine Arts*, Vienna: Academy of Fine Arts/Sternberg Press, pp. 138–147.

Bibliography

Allison, A. (1994), *Nightwork: Sexuality, Pleasure, and Corporate Masculinity in a Tokyo Hostess Club*, Chicago: University of Chicago Press.

Auslander, P. (2003), 'Good Old Rock and Roll: Performing the 1950s in the 1970s', *Journal of Popular Music Studies*, 15: 2, pp. 166–194.

Auslander, P. (1999), *Liveness: Performance in a Mediatized Culture*, London and New York: Routledge.

Auslander, P. (1996), 'Liveness: Performance and the Anxiety of Simulation', in Elin Diamond (ed.), *Performance and Cultural Politics*, London and New York: Routledge, pp. 196–213.

Auslander, P. (2006), *Performing Glam Rock: Gender and Theatricality in Popular Music*, Ann Arbor: University of Michigan Press.

Barthes, R. (1977), *Image/Music/Text*, S. Heath (trans.), New York: Hill & Wang.

Baudrillard, J. (1994), *Simulation and Simulacra*, Ann Arbor: University of Michigan Press.

Benedict, R. (1946), *The Chrysanthemum and the Sword: Patterns of Japanese Culture*, Boston: Houghton Mifflin Company.

Blacking, J. (1973), *How Musical is Man?*, Seattle and London: University of Washington Press.

Bourdieu, P. (1984), *Distinction: A Social Critique of the Judgment of Taste*, Cambridge: Harvard University Press.

Brooks, D. (2000), *Bobos in Paradise: The New Upper Class and How They Got There*, New York: Simon & Schuster.

Burns, L. and Lafrance, M. (2002), *Disruptive Divas: Feminism, Identity, and Popular Music*, London and New York: Routledge.

Butler, J. (1990), *Gender Trouble: Feminism and the Subversion of Identity*, London and New York: Routledge.

Butler, J. (2007), 'Performative Acts and Gender Constitution: An Essay in Phenomenology and Feminist Theory', in H. Bial (ed.), *The Performance Studies Reader*, 2nd edn, London and New York: Routledge, pp. 187–199.

Buxton, A. and Cornish, J. (2003), 'The Adam and Joe Show', *Adam and Joe Go Tokyo*, Episode 3, BBC 3, 13 June.

Case, S. (1989), 'Toward a Butch-Femme Aesthetic', in L. Hart (ed.), *Making a Spectacle: Feminist Essays on Contemporary Women's Theatre*, Ann Arbor: University of Michigan Press, pp. 295–297.

Cave, D. (2004), '"Sweet Caroline" Never Seemed So Good: So Uncool That It's Hip, Karaoke Enjoys a Comeback', *New York Times* (14 July), http://query.nytimes.com/gst/fullpage.html?res=9B0CE6DA163AF937A25754C0A9629C8B63, Accessed 20 February 2015.

Conquergood, D. (1992), 'Rethinking Ethnography: Toward a Critical Cultural Politics', *Quarterly Journal of Speech*, 78, pp. 80–97.

Crane, D. (1992), *The Production of Culture: Media and the Urban Arts*, Newbury Park: Sage Publications.

Cusic, D. (1991), 'Karaoke: High Tech and the Folk Tradition', *Tennessee Folklore Society Bulletin*, 55, pp. 51–55.

De Beauvoir, S. (1973), *The Second Sex*, New York: Vintage Books.

De Nora, T. (2000), *Music in Everyday Life*, Cambridge: Cambridge University Press.

Derrida, J. (1978), *Writing and Difference*, A. Bass (trans.), Chicago: University of Chicago Press.

de Waal, F. (1989), *Chimpanzee Politics: Power and Sex Among Apes*, Baltimore and London: Johns Hopkins University Press.

Drew, R. (2001), *Karaoke Nights: An Ethnographic Rhapsody*, Walnut Creek: Alta Mira Press.

Drew, R. (2005), 'Once More, With Irony: Karaoke and Social Class', *Leisure Studies*, 24: 4, pp. 371–383.

Drew, R. (2004), '"Scenes" Dimensions of Karaoke in the United States', in A. Bennett and R. A. Peterson (eds.), *Music Scenes: Local, Translocal and Virtual*, Nashville: Vanderbilt University Press, pp. 64–79.

Dyer, R. (1990), 'In Defense of Disco', in S. Frith and A. Goodwin (eds.), *On Record: Rock, Pop, and the Written Word*, New York: Pantheon Books, pp. 410–418.

Ehrenreich, B. (2006), *Dancing in the Streets: A History of Collective Joy*, New York: Henry Holt and Company.

Ehrenreich, B. (2001), *Nickel and Dimed: On (not) Getting by in America*, New York: Metropolitan.

Fine, E. C. and Speer, J. H. (1992), 'Introduction', in E. C. Fine and J. H. Speer (eds.), *Performance, Culture, and Identity*, Westport and London: Praeger, pp. 1–22.

Fish, S. (1980), *Is There a Text in this Class?*, Cambridge: Harvard University Press.

Fite, A. A. (n.d.), 'F.A.Q.' *Anastasia's Movieoke*, http://www.movieoke.net/faq.htm, Accessed 10 December 2007.

Fornäs, J. (1994), 'Karaoke: Subjectivity, Play and Interactive Media', *Nordicom Review*, 15: 1, pp. 87–103.

Fornäs, J. (1998), 'Filling Voids Along the Byway: Identification and Interpretation in the Swedish Forms of Karaoke', in T. Mitsui and S. Hosokawa (eds.), *Karaoke Around the World: Global Technology, Local Singing*, London and New York: Routledge, pp. 115–131.

Foucault, M. (1977), *Discipline and Punish: The Birth of the Prison*, New York: Pantheon.

Frith, S. (1996), *Performing Rites: On the Value of Popular Music*, Cambridge: Harvard University Press.

Frith, S. (1981), *Sound Effects: Youth, Leisure, and the Politics of Rock 'n' Roll*, New York: Pantheon Books.

Frith, S. and McRobbie, A. (1990), 'Rock and Sexuality', in S. Frith and A. Goodwin (eds.), *On Record: Rock, Pop, and the Written Word*, New York: Pantheon Books, pp. 371–389.

Fritsch, I. (2003), 'A Yen for the Traditional: In Modern Japan, Street Performers Sell Ritual and Nostalgia to Compete with High-Tech Advertising', *Natural History*, 112: 4, pp. 48–51.

Gans, H. (1974), *Popular Culture and High Culture*, New York: Basic Books.

Garfinkel, Y. (2003), *Dancing at the Dawn of Agriculture*, Austin: University of Texas Press.

Garofalo, R. (1994), 'Culture Versus Commerce: The Marketing of Black Popular Music', *Public Culture*, 7: 1, pp. 275–288.

Garofalo, R. (1997), *Rockin' Out: Popular Music in the USA*, Needham Heights: Allyn & Bacon.

Geertz, C. (1973), *The Interpretation of Cultures*, New York: Basic Books.

Geertz, C. (1988), *Works and Lives: The Anthropologist as Author*, Stanford: Stanford University Press.

Gaulène, M. (2013), 'Karaoke in Japan is a Veritable Industry', INA Global (17 September), http://www.inaglobal.fr/en/music/article/karaoke-japan-veritable-industry, Accessed 20 February 2015.

Goffman, E. (1979), *Gender Advertisements*, New York: Harper & Row.

Goffman, E. (1959), *The Presentation of Self in Everyday Life*, New York: Doubleday.

Gonda, T. A. (1993), *Karaoke: The Bible: Everything You Need to Know About Karaoke*, Oakland: G-Man Publishing Company.

Gracyk, T. (1996), *Rhythm and Noise: An Aesthetics of Rock*, Durham: Duke University Press.

Grossberg, L. (1993), 'The Media Economy of Rock Culture: Cinema, Post-modernity, and Authenticity', in S. Frith, A. Goodwin, and L. Grossberg (eds.), *Sound and Vision: The Music Video Reader*, London and New York: Routledge, pp. 185–209.

Grossberg, L. (1992), *We Gotta Get Out of This Place: Popular Conservatism and Post-modern Culture*, London and New York: Routledge.

Horton, D. (1990), 'The Dialogue of Courtship in Popular Song', in S. Frith and A. Goodwin (eds.), *On Record: Rock, Pop, and the Written Word*, New York: Pantheon Books, pp. 14–26.

Husserl, E. (1962), *Ideas: General Introduction to Pure Phenomenology*, B. Gibson (trans.), London: Collier-MacMillan.

Iyer, P. (1999), 'Daisuke Inoue The Karaoke King', *Time* [Asia], 154: 7/8 (23–30 August), http://www.time.com/time/asia/asia/magazine/1999/990823/inoue1.html, Accessed 20 February 2015.

Jackson Jr., J. L. (2005), *Real Black: Adventures in Racial Sincerity*, Chicago: University of Chicago Press.

Jones, S. (1992), *Rock Formation: Music, Technology, and Mass Communication*, Newbury Park: Sage.

Kelly, R. D. G. (1994), *Race Rebels: Culture, Politics, and the Black Working Class*, New York: The Free Press.

Kelly, W. H. (1997), *Empty Orchestras: an Anthropological Analysis of Karaoke in Japan*, Doctoral Thesis, The University of Oxford.

Kelly, W. H. (2002), 'Training for Leisure: Karaoke and the Seriousness of Play in Japan', in J. Hendry and M. Raveri (eds.), *Japan at Play: The Ludic and the Logic of Power*, London and New York: Routledge, pp. 152–168.

Keil, C. (1994), 'Music Mediated and Live in Japan', *Ethnomusicology*, 28: 1 (1984), 91–96, Reprinted in C. Keil and S. Feld (eds.), *Music Grooves*, Chicago: University of Chicago Press, pp. 247–256.

Kondo, D. (1990), *Crafting Selves: Power, Gender, and Discourses of Identity in a Japanese Workplace*, Chicago: University of Chicago Press.

Levine, L. (1988), *Highbrow/Lowbrow: The Emergence of Cultural Hierarchy in America*, Cambridge and London: Harvard University Press.

Lum, C. M. K. (1996), *In Search of a Voice: Karaoke and the Construction of Identity in Chinese America*, Mahwah: L. Erlbaum Associates.

McNeill, D. (2006), 'The Man Who Taught the World to Sing', *Independent*, Independent News and Media Limited, 25 May, http://news.independent.co.uk/world/asia/article570945.ece, Accessed 21 August 2007.

Maruyama, K. (1991), *Hito-wa naze utau-noka* [Why Do Humans Sing?], Tokyo: Asuka-shinsa.

Merleau-Ponty, M. (1962), *Phenomenology of Perception*, C. Smith (trans.), New York: Humanities Press.

Mitsui, T. (1998), 'The Genesis of Karaoke: How the Combination of Technology and Music Evolved', in T. Mitsui and S. Hosokawa (eds.), *Karaoke Around the World: Global Technology, Local Singing*, London and New York: Routledge, pp. 31–41.

Moorehead, A. (1966), *The Fatal Impact: An Account of the Invasion of the South Pacific, 1767–1840*, New York: Harper & Row.

n.a. (1993), 'Jōshi, Sempai, Okyokusama ni Kirawarenai: Karaoke Jū Jō', *Josei Seben* (22 April), pp. 64–67.

n.a. (2008), 'Karaoke Booms As Recession Bites', *PRLog* (20 November), http://www.prlog.org/10143999-karaoke-booms-as-recession-bites.html, Accessed 20 February 2015.

n.a. (2004), 'Karaoke's Creator Wins Ig Nobel Prize', *National Public Radio*, 1 October 2004.

n.a. (2004), 'Karaokes, Recording Companies in Discord Over Music Videos' Copyright', *China Daily* (11 October), p. 5.

Negus, K. (1992), *Music Genres and Corporate Cultures*, London and New York: Routledge, 1999.

Newsweek Staff (1992), 'It's Time to Maim That Tune', *Newsweek* (29 June), p. 57.

Said, E. W. (1979), *Orientalism*, New York: Vintage.

Onishi, N. (2010), 'Sinatra Song Often Strikes Deadly Chord', *New York Times* (6 February), p. A6.

O'Reilly, T. (2005), 'What Is Web 2.0: Design Patterns and Business Models for the Next Generation of Software', O'Reilly Media, 30 September, http://oreilly.com/pub/a/web2/archive/what-is-web-20.html, Accessed 20 February 2015.

Padel, R. (2000), *I'm a Man: Sex, Gods and Rock 'n' Roll*, London: Faber and Faber.

Paoletti, J. B. (2012), *Pink and Blue: Telling the Girls From the Boys in America*, Bloomington: Indiana University Press.

Putnam, R. D. (2000), *Bowling Alone: The Collapse and Revival of American Community*, New York: Simon & Schuster.

Raftery, B. (2008), *Don't Stop Believin': How Karaoke Conquered the World and Changed My Life*, Cambridge: De Capo Press.

Redmond, M. (1998), 'Karaoke Fans Capable of Killing More Than Tunes', *Indianapolis Star* (16 December), p. E1.

Reynolds, S. and Press, J. (1995), *The Sex Revolts: Gender, Rebellion, and Rock 'n' Roll*, Cambridge: Harvard University Press.

Rufus, A. (1993), 'Introduction to Karaoke: Into the Limelight', in T. A. Gonda (ed.), *Karaoke: The Bible: Everything You Need to Know About Karaoke*, Oakland: G-Man Publishing Company, pp. 19–22.

Sanjek, D. (1997), 'One Size Does Not Fit All: The Precarious Position of the African-American Entrepreneur in Post WW2 American Popular Music', *American Music*, 15: 4, pp. 535–562.

Seabrook, J. (2001), *Nobrow: The Culture of Marketing and the Marketing of Culture*, New York: Random House.

Shirai, S. (1997), *Karaoke: Sing Along Guide to Fun & Confidence*, Honolulu: Visual Perspectives.

Smitherman, G. (1977), *Talkin and Testifyin: The Language of Black America*, Detroit: Wayne State University Press.

Stokes, M. (1994), 'Introduction: Ethnicity, Identity and Music', in M. Stokes (ed.), *Ethnicity, Identity and Music: The Musical Construction of Place*, Oxford and New York: Berg Publishers, pp. 1–27.

Stoute, L. (1995), 'Curtains for Clintons: Breeding Ground for New Talent Switches to Karaoke Format', *Toronto Star* (7 December), p. H7.

Wong, D. (1994), '"I Want the Microphone": Mass Mediation and Agency in Asian-American Popular Music', *The Drama Review*, 38: 3, pp. 152–167.

Xun, Z. and Tarocco, F. (2007), *Karaoke: The Global Phenomenon*, London: Reaktion Books.

Index

www.ingramcontent.com/pod-product-compliance
Lightning Source LLC
LaVergne TN
LVHW060728310826
846742LV00016B/54
* 9 7 8 1 7 8 3 2 0 4 4 4 1 *